Also by Tito Alquizola

Return Flight and Other Essays (2004)

journeys
The Santo Niño Devotion
Comes to Tampa Bay

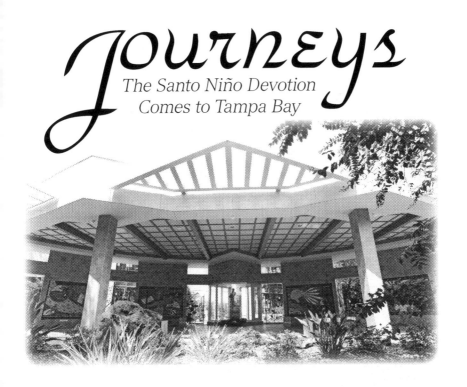

Tito Alquizola

iUniverse, Inc.
Bloomington

iUniverse books may be ordered through booksellers or by contacting:

iUniverse
1663 Liberty Drive
Bloomington, IN 47403
www.iuniverse.com
1-800-Authors (1-800-288-4677)

ISBN: 978-1-4620-6992-7 (sc)
ISBN: 978-1-4620-6994-1 (hc)
ISBN: 978-1-4620-6993-4 (ebook)

Cover: The Santo Niño Statue at the Shrine
Edited by Lucienne Alquizola
Author's Picture: Ireneo Racoma
All photographs: Tito Alquizola

Printed in the United States of America

iUniverse rev. date: 12/02/2011

To All Devotees of the Santo Niño

To Father Leonard Piotrowski,
Pastor, St. Paul Church, Tampa, Florida

and

To Lily, Vincent and Neil Alquizola

The Officers and Members of the Santo Niño Shrine USA express their deep appreciation to Everyone who has supported the Santo Niño Devotion through the years. May the Blessings of the Santo Niño be with you always.

Acknowledgements

The author is most grateful to the following individuals for graciously giving me their precious time to talk about their stories, their recollections and their views on being part of the Santo Niño Devotion –

Tito and Nilda dela Cruz, Ledy Colina, Deacon Max and Chit Montayre, Jose and Maria Raffiñan, Ed and Susan Bilbao, Marilyn Navarro, Fatima Dompor, Ben Mosquera, Romeo Gador, Raxtie Auza, Adela Gianan, Alice Kuntz, Father Jose Colina, Carmen Co, Antonio and Vilma Bayani, Lisa Kenyon, Thelma Mix, Laura Kuechenberg, Magda and Alberto Portela, Anne Marie Kearney, Mercie Bilbao, Ireneo and Helen Racoma, Rolly and Connie Barcenilla, Rene and Evelyn Bondoc, TQ Solis, Joey Omila, Teresa and Mel Ebrada, Sylvia Gogo, Esther Gianan and a lady named Tranquilina. Their stories are the heart and soul of this book.

———————————————

A very special thanks, (and a new bottle of aspirin), to my daughter, Lucy Alquizola, for the hours she spent restoring coherence and basic sense to my recurring run-away prose.

A gloriously pixelated thanks to Daphne Auza for stealing time from her tight school schedule to design the book's cover.

Had I the heavens' embroidered cloths,

Enwrought with golden and silver light,

The blue and the dim and the dark cloths

Of night and light and the half-light,

I would spread the cloths under your feet:

But I, being poor, have only my dreams;

I have spread my dreams under your feet;

Tread softly because you tread on my dreams.

— **W. B. Yeats,** *He wishes for the Cloths of Heaven*

Contents

Author's Introduction

Friendships to Devotion to Family

We started as friends casually gathered to pray in a family's living room. Then we became a Devotion. We were a group of strangers seeking a sense of home. Then we became a Family.

Friendships to Devotion to Family – an evolution worth noting. Celebrating, even.

For that one person in the hazy, distant future, who might be curious about our Devotion and can still make sense of the printed word, here is that story.

∾

Everything that the Tampa Bay Santo Niño group did through the years was done as a Family. In the prayers on First Fridays, the voices are of a family praying together. In the raucousness and solemnities of Fiesta celebrations, we see a family reunion. In deaths, we have the intimacy of shared grief. In weddings and births, we see a family in jubilation.

Friendships and devotions however defy analysis. Like flowers and sunsets they just are. They are their own reason for being. They either happen or they don't.

The whys and wherefores of this evolution we cannot dare to tease out. We are made of many images. We are a picture of yearning, transported hearts. From another angle we are seen as kindreds struggling to put down roots. From another light we are believers searching for answered prayers. All that does not make for an instant, coherent tapestry.

Then there are those times of easy break-ups and dissolutions, when we get into relationships with a limited shelf–life. For many reasons, temporal and spiritual, the Santo Niño group survived that very human quirk of our growth and development. A gratifying thought indeed.

That we, a small group of emigrants, from devotional zeal and determination have erected a Shrine on a foreign land, a patch of earth which is not our birth-place, is reason for jubilation. We should not forget how rare a phenomenon that is. It is not every day, nor every twenty years, that a small, self-organized group of emigrants got together and built a monument to their beliefs and heritage. And this is not solely about us and for us alone. This is for everyone all over the world who shares our Beliefs.

For many, many lifetimes, this monument to the Santo Niño Devotion will stand to give peace and solace for generations to come. This became a reality because we became a Family, a Family with a Family project, a Family dream.

(We have to note here that the erection of the Shrine was largely made possible by the financial contribution of the Navarro-Bilbao Family).

❧

The word "devotion" evokes images of heads bowed in prayer, veiled faces, still shadows on church walls. It has the hum of prayers, the whispered pleas of many voices, the footsteps of pilgrims.

But the faces in a devotional crowd are indistinct, blurring into each other. Conversations with one's God are personal, intimate, whispered by the heart in softly lighted corners. Voices from unseen faces.

Our Family Home has many faces, instantly recognizable, vaguely familiar, faces radiating multi-cultural and multi-generational memories. We are now an assortment of these cultures and memories. Thus, the need to have a better feel of who we are.

Our Devotion was shaped with what we carried in our luggages, what we secreted in our hearts through our many journeys. It was built with the sum of our parts, which we turned over for spiritual safekeeping. It may take us some time to trace the physical and spiritual paths we have travelled. Sorting out the pieces of ourselves strewn on the trail of our journeys can be confusing.

The idea for this book was proposed to me by Ed Bilbao sometime in 2009. Initially, I was reluctant to do this book for personal and technical reasons. Most of my life was spent as a care-taker of temporal needs. My familiarity with the inner workings of devotion and the interior lives of devotees is next to nothing.

The story of the Santo Niño group is about people, about love and devotion; about personal and organizational causes, conflicts, crises, consolations, conversions; about attachments to the Divine, the Sacred and the mundane; about physical, emotional and spiritual journeys; about personal and group idiosyncrasies.

The significance, the width and breadth of the project overwhelmed me.

My writing career so far had dealt only with such subjects as the disorientation and ambivalence of immigrants, the blighted romances of AARP adolescents and the travails of a young physician as a circumcision expert in a Cebu small town.

My final decision to start writing this book was influenced largely by Ed's and Deacon Max's unwavering confidence that I could do the job, plus my wife Florenda and my daughter Lucy steadily clearing the brush and wild undergrowths of my mind so I can see where the path opens. They saved me from imploring in desperation the guidance of Saints Luke, Matthew, Mark and John, and every evangelist who had ever dipped a quill to a pot of ink.

The emotional orientation to write the book began with closely listening to the voices during the First Friday prayers and other Santo Niño solemnities, to the gaiety and the laughter at the fellowships. I roamed with and weaved through the crowds on Fiesta days and during the many Shrine celebrations in 2010. After doing the initial interviews and putting down some preparatory words, I still could not find the right voice to tell the Santo Niño Devotion stories.

This is a grand story of one singular devotion born in many places, in different times, in hot and in cold seasons, in war and in peace, in luxury and in poverty, in contentment and discontent, in physical, emotional and spiritual dislocations. It is native- born and foreign-born. It has stood still in one place. It has made many journeys. It carries the memories and faces of generations. The story needs a special tone, timbre and rhythm. It must be played in deeper, robust chords. I could not find any of those in me. My initial melody lacked resonance and my words were flat and pale.

∾

I decided to go to Cebu where the Santo Niño Devotion began. Florenda and I stayed for four weeks, as usual, in the comforts of Winnie and Lito Basa's home in Cebu City. Three times I went to the open-air, hourly Friday prayers and Mass at the Basilica Minore de Santo Niño in Cebu City. I stayed for hours with the endless crowd of devotees which filled the vast quadrangle of the Basilica from early morning to when the city lights turn on. All through the days I was at the Basilica, the Philippine sun was merciless.

I tried to absorb as much as I could. The murmured solicitations from long rows of candle vendors dressed in bright red and orange uniforms, there from morning to nightfall under the broiling sun, ceaselessly moving in gentle undulations like the papier mache dragon on Chinese New Year. The continuous chants of the endless Sinulog prayer offerers all over the vast grounds of the Basilica. The panorama of hundreds of devotees in silent prayer, lined in front of seemingly endless stretches of candle stands, their solemn faces glowing with the reflection from countless red candles. The enveloping hush inside the Basilica itself, the worshipping faces, always the faces, of hundreds of people standing in line on their way to make their murmured supplications to the image of the Santo Niño. Each day I was there, I tried to feel all that.

Then I went back many times to Barili, my hometown in Cebu, before and during Holy Week, watching the preparation of the 27 'caros' for the long procession depicting Christ's 'Passion'. The solemn procession at dusk of 'caros' carrying life-sized statues portraying various stages of Christ's torture, paraded chronologically to portray Christ's way to Calvary. On the faces of that endless crowd following the procession in my hometown,

I saw again the faces of the devotion I was raised in, something I have long forgotten.

Through our countless travels our sense of Devotion has changed its cultural and national orientation. Crossing and re-crossing seas and lands have tempered the timbre of our devotional voices and have altered our sense of friendship and family. In my own case, there was the need to go back to my hometown church to be with the faces and the voices that instilled and shaped the genetics of my beliefs. I had to go back to where my own devotional voice was initially tuned, where I had originally absorbed the nature of friendship and family. From all that and having *felt* the life-beat of the Santo Niño Basilica day in and day out, I found the initial notes to start this book's tune.

Becoming a Family in prayer has made us see the significant shadings of what we are as shaped by the sadness and joy, the defeats and triumphs of our lives. We are the distillate of our moments of reflection and distraction, of our states of belief and unbelief. This book attempts to tell our stories from which we hope to see a discernible portrait of our Family, a reasonable facsimile of our faces in this Devotion. As we see a fuller view of our faces, perhaps then we will eventually know our hearts. – Tito Alquizola, September 6, 2011

∽

Foreword

"God wants people to exercise their
freedom and love, and so he comes
as a child and displays not earthly
power, but the apparent
helplessness of his love"

Pope Benedict XVI

The Footprints of Our Journeys

by Ed A. Bilbao
President, Santo Niño Shrine USA

Stories are the colorful footprints of human existence. Verbally told or in print, stories comprise a kaleidoscope of countless individual journeys. They show a gamut of emotions with the innocence of the "mouth of babes" or the tempered sentiments of the aging. Stories make us cry, make us laugh, leave us amused. Struggles, sacrifices and feats of valor are clearly understood when knitted and woven into a tapestry of words that can be preserved for generations. Civilizations and social transformations are made clearer when told in story form. Stories can make us feel as though we've touched the divine as they make us truly human. This is what this book is all about. Prominently portrayed in these pages are many personal realities, faith in God and journeys in faith.

It is a source of great joy for me and my wife, Susan, to be given a once-in-a- lifetime opportunity to be a part of this book about the Filipino-American community in Tampa Bay. It captures a myriad of individual stories that beautifully portray the unique spiritual side of people in our area.

Inspired by the Catholic devotion to the Santo Niño (The Holy Child Jesus), little known in the United States but popular among Filipinos everywhere, *Journeys* relates the stories of people who found their own Santo Niño Devotion. The author, Tito Alquizola, shows in this book the colorful facets of people becoming The Devotion. We can also see a community of people whose lives are intertwined by common values and spirituality, gathered in prayer and social interaction. The writing is full of heart, pointing the reader to many kinds of intimate realities, as we find meaning in the mundane events of our everyday lives. In this book, the religiosity of Filipinos shows through in their communal prayers, especially in their devotion to the Santo Niño, the Child Jesus.

We deeply appreciate the efforts Tito has put into the research and writing of this book. His writing reveals the journalistic lessons he has learned as a young man in the Philippines who has been writing seriously since high school. He was Editor-in-Chief and feature writer in the University of San Carlos, Boy's High School publication, The Junior Carolinian. While a student at the University of Santo Tomas Medical School, Tito was associate editor and columnist of the Varsitarian, the UST publication. In the late 1950s, he published articles in the Manila Times Sunday Magazine, Philippines Herald Sunday Magazine, Women's Magazine and other Manila publications. Except for one short story published in the Philippine Free Press in 1967, Tito stopped publishing until the late 1990s when, for a year, he wrote a column for the Sunday Magazine of the Cebu SunStar, a newspaper published in Cebu City. The reason for the 30-year journalistic silence was his decision to focus on his fulltime psychiatric practice.

But he never stopped writing, he just did not publish what he wrote. "A writer can never stop writing", Tito says. The publication silence was broken in September 2004 when the UST Publishing House in Manila published Tito's collection of essays about immigrant life, *"Return Flight"*.

He has been blest in a 47-year marriage with Florenda "Flor" Alquizola, his co-graduate in the UST Medical School. They have three children and three grandchildren. Since 1992, when Tito and Florenda moved to Tampa from Cincinnati, both have been active participants of the Santo Niño Devotion. Flor remains active in the officer slate of Santo Nino Shrine organization.

My friendship with Tito spanned many years and many associations since he and Flor moved to Tampa. We had a connection in the past too, before Tampa Bay. Specially telling is our having finished our academic studies in the same school, the University of Santo Tomas. He, from the UST medical school while I finished college in the UST Seminary. In my time at Santo Tomas, it was not uncommon for UST seminarians to be involved in the secular life of the university. Because of my activities with the dramatic guild and other non-seminary programs, I had the privilege of having been chosen as one of the campus personalities featured in the Varsitarian, the publication where Tito honed his writing skills years before I came to UST.

A number of subjects in this book revolve around the planning and building of the Santo Niño Shrine and Prayer Space at the grounds of St. Paul Catholic Church in Tampa. It was built in July 2010, inaugurated in December 2010 and seen by the out-of-town devotees during the 2011 Fiesta. The building, which had been donated to the Catholic Diocese of St. Petersburg, is one of the tangible products of the community's Santo Niño Devotion, a religious prayer-group which has been together in Tampa Bay for twenty-three years.

In addition to my friendship with Tito, he has a warm closeness to the Devotion. In turn, he has gifted the Santo Niño community this fine book. I owe a debt of gratitude to Tito for his dogged determination to finish the book after treading many winding roads with people in the narratives that, I believe, had ultimately led them closer to God's grace. I also thank the many individuals who were so willing to tell the stories of their involvement with the Santo Niño Devotion and how their lives have been changed because of the Santo Niño Devotion. We also recall with fond memory those who had given a committed involvement to the Devotion through the years but have now joined their Maker.

In our prayers, we want them to know that the people they left behind have continued the unity and the fervor which they showed when they were still with us.

It is my hope that readers of this book will reflect on their personal spirituality and continuing "journeys to grace." To quote from the inscription in the Santo Nino Shrine, I pray that through this book "they may find solitude, peace and God."

— E. A. B., September 19, 2011

1

Another Glorious Day — 'Pit Senyor!'

It is late afternoon. The thick crowd which filled the St. Paul Church campus since early morning is thinning out. The day of another Santo Niño Fiesta is ending. But for everyone involved with the preparation of the Fiesta, there is a spreading mood of contentment that another celebration for countless Santo Niño devotees have taken place.

Echoes and after-images of the Fiesta continue to be heard and seen in the minds of the celebrants left on the parish grounds. It's like a loop of film that plays and plays the cacophony of gleeful, excited voices reverberating throughout the church campus all through the joyful day. The seemingly edgeless expanse of women in variously, fashionably designed red dresses, that special red reflecting the color of the Santo Niño cape. The men outfitted in quieter color schemes but just as festively dressed, with some in Filipino barongs also in Santo Niño red.

So many images the mind cannot stop replaying. The endless parade of people carrying a Santo Niño statue of varied sizes and costumes, walking to the church and to the newly opened Santo Niño Shrine. The Shrine, gleaming like a freshly unwrapped gift, left the crowd awed and amazed at its seemingly overnight appearance. The Santo Niño Shrine was received like a flower which blooms only once in so many generations. One can only wonder how far into the future can another Filipino generation build a shrine to a devotion they carry.

The replaying of the day's images continue.

The Offertory Dancers at the Family Center putting on their costumes while testing the suppleness of their dancing limbs, like newborn calves learning to walk. In some distant room the choir members are tuning their voices. The guest officiating bishop from the Philippines being toured around the campus by Father Joy Colina. The prelate nurses his jet lag with gracious ecclesiastical smiles for everyone he meets. Fleetingly seen, hurriedly weaving through and briefly greeting the incoming crowd, still in colorful non-liturgical outfit, is Father Len Piotrowski, the Pastor of St. Paul, walking his dog. A pet's basic needs attended to before its Master is swept into hours of festive pastoral activities.

At the Parish Pavilion, Helen, Ledy, Flora, Maria, Jun, Nilda, Tito, Charito, Chuck, Joe and Ellen, braving the early January morning cold, as they had been doing the past few Fiestas, setting up tables, chairs and food for the afternoon free banquet. Food coming in has to be meticulously checked for its freshness, for its promised quantity, including the series of lechon roasting a few feet away inside an improvised tent, tainting the ladies' cosmetic airs with the aroma of grilled pork. Helen Racoma, traversing the distance between the Pavilion and the Family Center, not once, not twice, but three or four times, to cook more rice. The Pavilion does not have an outlet for the rice cooker.

In the meantime, Josefina 'Pining' Raffinan and Chit Montayre are putting on the finishing touches of the altar decoration, always elegantly grand, as though a hundred springs have bloomed.

The church is filling up fast even if the celebratory Mass is still an hour and a half away. Devotees are spilling out into the sidewalks. Most stay at the Shrine, sitting on the gleaming granite benches, beside the expanding rows of variedly sized and costumed Santo Niño statues at the foot of the Shrine's main statue.

Then the hour, 12:30 arrives. The grand entrance of the Guest Bishop Celebrant, the long row of concelebrating priests, solemnly walking on the church aisle, in the middle of the Knights of Columbus Honor Guard. The Santo Niño Choir, led by Connie Chanrasmi, ushers the regal mood with a rousing hymn. The liturgical celebration begins.

After the Celebrant's homily on the intertwining of emigrant life and the carrying on of Filipino religious tradition, the Offertory Dancers under the direction of Joey Omila, momentarily turns the church aisle into a musical theatre stage. In stylish choreography, in glittery, blindingly colorful pre-Hispanic Filipino costumes, Omila's dancers recreate, in dance and drumbeats, the bestowing of the original Santo Niño statue to the royalty of Cebu in 1521. The multi-Filipino-language Prayer for the Faithful, (including

Spanish and English), recited by those who speak the particular Filipino language, takes the Mass to its grand ending. The Procession of the Santo Niño statue, winds around the tall Florida oaks of the St. Paul campus to the tune of simultaneously recited rosaries interweaving with the roar of the Dale Mabry traffic.

Then the swarming rush of the vast crowd to the banquet, the servers handing out food-filled plates with the skill and finesse of Chinese jugglers.

∽

All of that are over now. The film is at its final frame. Like a deep, prolonged sigh, quiet is slowly spreading over the church campus. Now and then, short bursts of distant delighted voices can be heard from small isolated groups in various corners of the campus, celebrants reluctant to end the day. Just as hesitant to leave the day is the Florida sun in Tampa Bay. It hovers over the horizon as though undecided where to start painting the sea in rich reddish orange.

The Fiesta colors are being packed away. The colored buntings taken down and rolled neatly. The vestments of the Bishop and the priests, in their glittering reds, greens and gold, now lay muted in the dark of diocesan closets. The dazzling reds, whites, purples and blues of the devotees' barongs and ternos are in the gloom of garment bags. The rainbow of the altar flowers, the dancers' costumes and every other kaleidoscopic hue that proclaim "Fiesta!" have faded with the darkening day.

Only the Florida sun and the red cape of the Santo Niño at the Shrine are left to blaze on the fading day.

In many dimmed corners inside St. Paul Church Family Center, small groups are still in energetic conversation, giving the cavernous place a steady hum. Garment bags with Fiesta clothes inside are carelessly tossed over the backs of chairs. The outfits have lost the crisp, immaculate sheen it had this morning. They are now richly adorned with wrinkles, with a variety of stains only a dry cleaning attendant can love.

The day's rush, excitement and programs to be executed with military precision are vividly illustrated with the graphics of dried perspiration, roast pork grease stains, grass, leaf and flower sap smudges, candle drippings on those packed away clothes. They are also seen in how the stiletto heels and men's party shoes are carelessly dashed whichever which way under disordered chairs. Most of all it is felt by the slouching bodies and propped up sore feet. Fatigued perhaps but buoyed up with exhilaration that the Santo Niño had been given another "successful" Fiesta. Not bad for something planned and organized every year in ten days.

For many years now, these worn-out but still bright-eyed groups inside St. Paul Family Center are the people who have been making the Fiestas run smoothly. They are the organizers and planners who patiently go through endless meetings, who get the food ordered and served on time, who put up the decorations and the flowers in various places, who get the dancers and the choir together and well-rehearsed, who tirelessly help Susan Bilbao solicit contributions to finance the programs. Their names are all over this book in its proper context. With them are the rarely recognized hundreds who do the small but crucial activities in the background to make a Fiesta celebration look like the way it did today.

∽

In the meantime, at the St. Paul Church Pavilion where the banquet "for the multitudes" was served, another crucial activity is going on.

The scraping and bumping sounds of metal on metal, on concrete floors, play a dissonant accompaniment to the soft hiss and crackle of big, bulging plastic bags being stuffed into trash cans. Tito de la Cruz and Edgar 'Chuck' Kunzt, with their small army of helpers, are putting back in place the heavy tables and chairs, and neatly putting into trash bags tons of left-over food. After they have rendered the Pavilion spotless, the tables and chairs aligned as though with a ruler, it is difficult to imagine that just a few hours ago, a seemingly endless surge of people from all over Florida and other states were fed in an orderly manner.

Through the years, the considerable effort spent in planning and preparing, (and raising funds), to get together this free luncheon for hundreds of Fiesta attendees have become a challenging enterprise. Placing the various food selections in place to make the serving more orderly already needs the talents of a military strategist. And that is done hours ahead by members of the Food Committee in red aprons draped over Fiesta outfits. The luncheon's actual serving is a combination of cafeteria work, crowd control and directing traffic on Hillsborough Avenue. Through the years the names of Charito Raffinan, Nilda de la Cruz, Dolores Mosquera, Fatima Dompor, Maria Raffinan, Ledy Colina, Helen Racoma, Flor Alquizola, Zeny Cruz, Vilma Bayani, Jose and Ellen Padilla and many, many more have been closely associated with this crucial Fiesta activity. It has become a permanent assignment every year for this group of people who have been in the organization almost from the very beginning. It goes all the way back to the days in the mid to the late 1990s when the "feeding of the multitudes" were done under "circus tents" put up yearly by Jose 'Jun' Raffinan, Tito de la Cruz,'Chuck' Kuntz, Joselito Reynes and their army of muscled helpers.

Spiritually intentioned as the organization is, the members also have a keen sense of reality that the corporeal needs of the Fiesta attendees, (say, a decent lunch), have to be attended to. What started as a simple pot-luck lunch at Kate Jackson Park in 1990, has evolved into a full-blown banquet.

These last hours are for savoring the day's joys and solemnities. To replay in the celebrants' minds the echoing voices singing the liturgical hymns, to feel in their limbs once more the movements of the Sinulog dances, to find a corner in their hearts and minds to keep today's devotional words. Then, to raise their voices once more the traditional cheer to the Santo Niño -- "Pit Senyor!"

2

Seeking a Second Shore

At the height of the Fiesta activities today, he intentionally placed himself in the middle of the milling crowd. He did not want anyone to recognize him, to know that he was back. He worried all day what he would do if someone took a closer look and recognize him. He was not ready to face them.

He walks slower now though, extra careful where his feet land. No more those brisk, confident, long strides. That's the walk they would connect with him. The day is ending and, as far as he knows, nobody has recognized him. Which is what he hoped, all day.

He is walking towards the Santo Niño Shrine. The St. Paul Church campus is almost deserted. The Sinulog dancers are lingering by their cars at the emptying parking lot. Their laughter floats beside him like an attentive friend. The dancers are reluctant to part from each other, continuing to talk about the day's excitement. The cheery voices from the parking lot brings a faint smile to this walking man's face. Briefly, his brightening face reveals that the voices and the laughter bring back some memory.

He steals a glance at the dancers. He cannot ignore their echoing laughter. Their bright red, green, gold costumes flicker with their movements, enriching the fading colors of the sun-setting day. Their interweaving Cebuano, English, Tagalog conversations give a faster rhythmic counterpoint to the man's measured walk towards the Santo Niño Shrine.

As he approaches, he sees the Shrine suffusing a soft glow to its surroundings. The darkness of the Florida oaks stops at the edges of the Shrine's brightness like a nocturnal creature backing away. The man feels the descending January chill.

He sits on the granite bench slightly to the side of the glass-enclosed Santo Niño statue. He looks at each of the mosaics. He feels a stillness, a sense of peace he has not felt for a long time. His many surges of feelings today had been difficult to hold back.

∽

For most of his life, he has perfected the skill of controlling the expression of his feelings. He can work at it with the precision of an expensive time piece. When to show emotions, and how much to show, is a discipline he has perfected throughout his life. He has always been afraid of being swept away in a flood of emotions. Such finely tuned self-discipline has led people to think of him as cold-hearted or indifferent.

At the Mass today, during the procession and the blessing of the Shrine by the Bishop, he tried his best to lose himself in the crowd. He does not feel ready to face his old friends, to let them know he has returned. The emotions might be too much.

He knows that he does not have to explain anything. From what he knew of these friends in the past, he is sure they are not the kind who asks for explanations. But still, something is bound to be said about his sudden disappearance eight years ago. And now, his sudden appearance. He does not even know himself why he came back.

Earlier, he could not help but join the cleaning crew at the Banquet Pavilion. In the early years as an active organizing member of the Santo Niño Devotion, he always volunteered to lead the cleaning crew at every Fiesta and First Friday Fellowships. He believed then that pure physical activity can be part of worship. He still does.

When he helped to clean up at the Pavilion today, he pulled down his cap to hide part of his face. He stayed in the far periphery, taking the full bulky trash bags to the dumpsters, working with young people who were not around eight years ago. He kept his distance and averted his face from those who might recognize him. Nobody recognized him. His eight-year absence has given him the looks of a stranger.

∽

It is almost unbelievable to think that he was very much a part of this Santo Niño Devotion when it was a simple house-to-house, informal prayer group in 1989. Bonded in prayer, in the togetherness of those seeking new places to call home, a closeness quickly developed between everyone.

Yet, without notice, without goodbyes, without a single word to hint what he was going to do, he left these prayer companions abruptly eight years ago. He isolated himself in a small bamboo house on a hollow between two small hills outside his hometown in the Philippines. He tried to erase from memory all his personal and professional successes in the United States. He went back to the Philippines not to die but to recapture some life, some vital fragment of lost innocence.

Living on that hollow alone, what he could never block out from his memory were the recurring times of togetherness he had with everyone in the early days of the Santo Niño Devotion.

Today he noted on the Fiesta Program that this is the 23rd Annual Santo Niño Fiesta Celebration. Twenty-third!

How vivid still in his mind that first, that *very* first, formally organized Fiesta Celebration. It was the third Sunday in January 1990. Under that fierce Florida sun, he and that pioneer Santo Niño group gathered on the dusty grounds of some partly developed public park somewhere in South Tampa. It was a festivity patched together with ideas tossed in casually, intermittently. There was no grand vision. There was only a fervent, unspoken feeling in everyone to be together in prayer.

On that hot, dusty grounds, a Devotion was born.

Now, all alone inside this Santo Niño Shrine, he feels that dream fulfilled. He imagines how filled with pride and gratitude his friends from 1990 must feel today seeing their vision turned into this solid glowing structure. Once upon a time he was one of the dreamers.

∽

The traffic on Dale Mabry has toned down to a muffled roar. It has gotten dark. All the street lights are on. He does not know how much time has passed. He wonders whether he has been praying during the long moments that have passed. He is only aware of having been lost in a world of thoughts.

Maybe getting lost in his thoughts is how he prays these days.

All his life he has been told that everything about our lives — our memories, our hurts, our joys, our loves, our hates, our successes, our failures, our exclamations, our

silences -- can be offered to God. For sometime now, especially this past eight years, when he completely isolated himself, whatever is left in his life he sees as a huge bouquet of withered flowers. Right here, at the foot of the Santo Niño statue, he still holds the hope that his imagined bouquet of withered flowers can have a place in anyone's altar. He has not given up on absolution. But right now, all that matters to him is the simple purity of the quiet and peace of being here.

The night deepens. The darkness outside makes the quiet feel solid as though a curtain has dropped around him. The passing cars on Dale Mabry are few and far between, muted in their passing. Even at this late hour, people are going places, leaving places. Journeys, this is what it's all about. This is what *we* are all about. His own journey? Who knows. He gazes intently at the brightly lighted Santo Niño statue...

∾

3

From Atocha to a Sense of Home

As that man in the Shrine realizes, taking journeys is what this is all about, what being of this world is all about. From the Philippines we have taken many journeys, and most of the time, in our luggage and in our hearts, we brought the Santo Niño. But centuries before our journeys, the Santo Niño had already been traveling. That is how He came to us in the first place, carried by men in search of spice and other condiments. Here is how His travel probably began.

Sometime in the 13th century, the town of Atocha in Spain was lost in battle to the Moors. All Christians were taken prisoner. Adults were not allowed to bring food or water to the prisoners. Out of nowhere, a small child dressed like a 13th century pilgrim, carrying a bag of food and a jug of water, started appearing at the prison camp. Since he was a child, the guards allowed him to give food and drink to the prisoners. It was soon noticed that no matter how many prisoners ate and drank, the child's bag of food and jug of water never emptied. After sometime, the people of Atocha saw this child with food and water as an apparition of the Child Jesus. As the veneration began, a small statue of the Child Jesus was soon erected and that became the devotion to the Child of Atocha. This is one of the earliest recorded devotions to the Child Jesus -- the Niño de Atocha (Child of Atocha).

The devotion to the Holy Child Jesus, a veneration of Christ's sacred Infancy, has been a tradition of the Catholic Church for centuries. Many saints had a very strong devotion to the Divine Child, notably St. Therese of the Child Jesus, St. Francis of Assisi, St. Anthony of Padua and St. Teresa of Avila.

The history of the Infant Jesus of Prague started in the 17th century when a statue of the Infant Jesus was brought into Bohemia (now the Czech Republic). It was then given to the Discalced Carmelites in Prague, the capitol city of the Czech Republic.

The exact origin of the Infant Jesus statue was not truly known, but historical sources point to a small 28-centimeter high sculpture of the Holy Child with a bird in his right hand, said to be carved around the year 1340. Many other Infant Jesus sculptures were also carved by artists throughout Europe in the Middle Ages. The appearance of some of these statues were reputedly based on the visions of St. Teresa of Avila.

Some of the sculptures which found its way to Prague were made in Spain. They were made of wax, ivory and bronze and dressed in garments reflecting the aristocratic fashion of that period. Such costumes are very similar to the "royal" vestments which Filipinos frequently dress their Santo Niño statues, a favorite conception of the Child Jesus as a Child Prince.

The exact origin of the statue which started to be venerated as the Infant Jesus of Prague is unknown. There were speculations that it came from a monastery in Bohemia, later obtained by Dona Isabella Manrique who gave it as a wedding gift to her daughter Marie Manrique, who married a noble of the Czech kingdom. Later, in 1587, the Holy Infant statue was given in turn to Marie's daughter Polyxena as a wedding gift. When Lady Polyxena's husband died in 1623, she decided to live a life of piety and charity, continually generous to the Carmelite priest and brothers of Prague. In 1628, Lady Polyxena presented the statue to the Carmelites at the Church of the Virgin Mary the Victorious in Mala Strana. In giving the statue, Lady Polyxena reputedly said -- "I am giving you my most prized possession. As long as you venerate this image you will not be in want." This statue became the fabled Infant Jesus of Prague. It is described in Catholic historical writings as "19 inches in height, encased in a royal mantle with a jeweled crown, its right hand raised in blessing, its left hand holding a globe signifying sovereignty."

To this day the statue of the Infant Jesus of Prague is where Lady Polyxena gave it in 1628 -- at the Church of the Virgin Mary Victorious, (built in 1611), in Mala Strana, at the foothills of the Prague castle, a town founded in 1257.

This bit of history implies that the devotion to the Holy Child of Atocha in 13th century Spain and other Holy Child devotions spreading all over Europe in the 1600s was the prevailing devotional atmosphere when Magellan left Spain in 1520 to do his circumnavigation. This might explain why of all the many devotional images he could have brought with him, he chose the statue of the Child Jesus, (later to become the Santo Niño de Cebu), as a symbol of the Christianity that Spain wanted to propagate.

From the stories of the Child of Atocha, to that of the Holy Child of Prague, all the way to the countless stories about the Philippine Santo Niño, the history of devotion unfolds from the travels of its images. In our endless journeys from unbelief to belief, from earthly preoccupations to a glimmer of the sublime, we somehow stumble across these devotional trails, endlessly blazing from century to century to century.

Wherever our destinations are, our devotional images are there. From the Magellan-bestowed Santo Niño statue now at the Basilica de Santo Niño de Cebu in Cebu City, Philippines, to the countless Santo Niño images in Filipino homes in the Philippines and all over the world, to the Santo Niño at the Shrine at St. Paul church in Tampa Florida, the Santo Niño image is ever present to give devotees, emigrants and non-emigrants, a Sense of Home.

4

Embers of a Burnt House, Fire of Devotion

On April 28, 1565, in a small village in the Philippines called Sugbu, (the Cebu City of today), out of the violence of foreign invaders, a priceless gift given to the Philippines some forty-four years earlier, was accidentally recovered. The gift had been laid aside or forgotten in the confusion of war. Once found again, it turned into a Devotion to which countless Filipinos have dedicated themselves for centuries now. Rarely have the spoils of war yielded a vessel for the salvation of human kind.

The battle that raged on that day was brought about by the return of another Spanish expedition led this time by Miguel Lopez de Legazpi. The Sugbu natives were not as friendly this time as they had been forty-four years earlier when the first Spanish-Portuguese expedition came with Magellan. Having killed Magellan in 1521, and brutalized by strangers from other lands through the succeeding years, the Filipinos were not as graciously welcoming in 1565. They were ready with their spears, poisoned arrows and machetes.

In the ensuing battle, the Spaniards burned the houses along their path. In one burning Sugbu house, a man named Juan Camus found in a pine box a carved statue of a child. The statue was not affected by the fire but slightly darkened by the heat and the smoke. Camus was a sailor in Legazpi's crew. As a Catholic, Camus knew this was not just another carved statue of a child. He recognized it as the statue of the Infant Jesus.

What Camus did not know was that this was the very statue given as a gift to the rulers of Cebu some forty-four years earlier when the rulers were baptized. An authenticated 1521 entry in the

13

journal of Antonio Pigafetta, a clerk and diarist of the Magellan expedition, stated that the statue of the Infant Jesus was presented to the wife of the chieftain of Cebu after her baptism by Father Pedro Valderrama, the chaplain of the Magellan expedition. The chieftain's queen was given the baptismal name of Juana after the Spanish Emperor's mother, Juana the Mad.

In Laurence Bergreen's book about Magellan's "Circumnavigation of the Globe" (Over the Edge of the World, Perennial-HarperCollins, 2003) is this quote from Pigafetta's diary —

"We conducted her (the Cebu chieftain's wife) to the platform, and she was made to sit down upon a cushion…She was shown an image of our Lady, *a very beautiful wooden child Jesus*, and a cross. Thereupon, she was overcome with contrition, and asked for baptism amid her tears."

Upon the discovery of this statue of the Child Jesus, Legazpi ordered an official inquiry which resulted in the official documentation that the statue came from Europe. This document was drawn on May 16, 1565 and is in the archives of the Santo Niño convent in Cebu, Philippines. The document consists of eyewitness accounts stating that the image was found in a small pine box, preserved in almost perfect condition with two fingers of its right hand raised in blessing, and the left hand holding an orb symbolizing the world.

∾

Once the statue's historical significance was fully recognized, it was entrusted to the Augustinian Missionaries. A church was built on the exact location where the statue was found. Since then the Augustinian Fathers were charged with the statue's keeping and the initiation and propagation of the Santo Niño Devotion. The Devotion rapidly spread throughout the entire island of Cebu and the whole country. To this day, wherever Filipinos are situated all over the world, there is a Santo Niño Devotion.

At the time of Magellan's arrival in the Philippines in 1521, the Child Jesus was widely venerated by Catholics all over Europe. The Santo Niño statue was the embodiment of Magellan's personal goodwill towards the Cebu royalty. But what started as a personal gift from Magellan took on a much larger significance -- the conversion of a large segment of the population to Catholicism. The baptism of a ruling couple became the baptism of a whole nation. That orb balanced on the Santo Niño statue's left hand is emblematic of the Catholic world which the Philippines entered.

In 1965 the interior of this historic Cebu City church, known at that time as San Agustin church, was renovated in observance of the 4th Centennial of the Christianization of the Philippines celebrated in Cebu City. During this celebration the church was elevated to the status of Basilica Minore de Santo Niño de Cebu by the Sacred Congregation of Rites in Rome.

Among Filipinos all over the world, the awareness about the Santo Niño Devotion ranges from those with a vague idea of it to those who grew up with it as a fervently observed family devotion. In these families, the Devotion is handed down through generations like a spiritual heirloom. These are the sons and daughters with indelible memories of growing up among grandparents and parents faithfully doing the nine-day novena every January. In their lifetime they have gone to Cebu City many times to participate in the festivities and have vivid memories of the crowds celebrating the January Fiesta. They have attended more than one High Mass inside the church packed with devotees. They have been mesmerized by the conflagration of candles around the San Agustin Church, (now the Basilica Minore). They have danced with endless rows of people doing the Sinulog outside and inside the church.

Some recall unusual ways of marking the feast. There is the daughter who remembers her father weighing an underweight, sickly brother. Then he buys enough candles with the same weight as his son which he then lights simultaneously during the Fiesta. The father believes that the candle flames carry the father's plea for the son to gain weight and be healthier.

Others remember hundreds of devotees from towns distant from Cebu City, or from the neighboring Visayan islands and Mindanao, arriving in Cebu City for the January fiesta. For those with relatives in Cebu City, the attendance to the Fiesta also serves as an annual family reunion. Those who do not have relatives or friends in the city who can provide lodging and cannot afford hotels, camp on the sidewalks around the Basilica. They smoke, they brew hot chocolate, they exchange stories about the special favors they have received from the Santo Niño. In the telling these favors are inevitably seen as small miracles. Since there is always someone with a guitar, they sing the night away until the first Mass in the morning. It has become proverbial that if you get two Cebuanos and a guitar together, you have a concert.

This kind of observance is very much what it is today. It has only become bigger. These days every Friday at the Basilica, there is a widely attended outdoor Mass every hour from early morning to dusk. Candle vendors in bright red-and-orange skirt and blouse, pants and shirt, line the quadrangle. On the grounds of the Basilica is a long row of tiered candle holders where even in the brightness of noon, the somber faces of praying devotees reflect the rich red of the candle flames. By the side entrance to the Basilica is the kiosk housing what is known as the Magellan Cross. That supposedly is the very spot where the first Catholic Mass in Cebu was celebrated in 1521. Inside the kiosk devotees dance the Sinulog.

On this ground the size of a city block, in the middle of Cebu City's old business district, Philippine Catholicism was born.

5

From a Broken Tree, a Sacred Image

The Belief that was narrowly bestowed to a royal family almost five centuries ago has now become a devotion which millions of Filipinos observe. Like those Portuguese and Spanish circumnavigators who accidentally, literally, ran aground on the islands now known as the Philippines, the Filipinos themselves are now circumnavigating the world.

One of the places the Filipinos have arrived at is that large patch of the world called America. In there is a longish piece of land called Florida which sticks out to the sea like an accusing finger. On the middle node of that finger is a city called Tampa which reputedly means "sticks of fire" in the language of the Calusa, a Native American tribe. In the southern part of Tampa, bordered with fashionable homes built in the 1950s and early 1960s, is a dusty city park named Kate Jackson. On the third Sunday in January 1990, a number of Tampa Bay devotees of the Santo Niño gathered there to celebrate their first organized Santo Niño Fiesta.

Towards the end of that year, November 1990, a catastrophic typhoon, (named "Ruping"), ravaged the Philippines. It left a devastating destruction of lives, property and natural resources. Twenty-years later in 2010, those two seemingly unrelated events in January and November 1990, occurring in opposite sides of the planet, became one crucial milestone on the long road to the Santo Niño Shrine: the donation of the Santo Niño statue to the Shrine by Carmen and Demosthenes Co. The 1628 tradition of Lady Polyxena of Prague lives on.

Here is how the January 1990 Kate Jackson Park Fiesta intertwine with the November 1990 Philippine typhoon.

∽

Carmen Co and Lolita Delgra, (Galvez sisters before their marriages), both physicians, grew up in Cebu City. For as long as both can remember, they were raised in the rich air of the annual Santo Niño festivities every January. The Fiesta was as marked in their lives as Christmas and their birthdays. Carmen remembers her late mother, Catalina, buying candles days before the Cebu Fiesta, then, with her sister, handing those candles to those without candles in the Santo Niño procession. She was doing this since the age of 7. About that time, her mother ordered from Spain a life-sized statue of the resurrected Jesus, which for years was used in the dawn procession for Easter Sunday in Cebu City.

When Carmen was 12 years old, the family moved to a new house. In front of the house was a small santol tree which simultaneously grew with Carmen and Lolita. A mature santol tree easily reaches 50 to 150 feet, with a big sturdy trunk. The santol tree (scientific name: *sandoricum koetjape* or *sandoricum indicum*) is a widely growing fruit and lumber tree in Asia. Its fruit is round with a bright orange-light-brown pulpy skin with a fine fuzz. When ripe, it has a gelatinous sweet-sour meat, popularly eaten in the Philippines. (see picture end of chapter).

When the Galvez' santol tree was bigger it became the sisters' favourite tree to climb and its branches to sit on. The tree became more popular for the sisters and their friends to congregate around when it started bearing fruit, everyone enjoying the juicy sweet-sour flavour of its fruit. To this day, Carmen and Lolita associate that santol tree with whatever was fun in their preteen and teen years.

In November 1990, Typhoon "Ruping" tore and twisted the tree's sturdy branches and uprooted that santol tree. By this time Carmen and Lolita, now wives, mothers and physicians, have already been residing in the United States for years. Carmen's mother Catalina could not see her fallen santol tree cut into pieces for fuel in bakery and restaurant kitchens. The tree was too much a part of the family as the play center of her daughters and their friends long ago. For Carmen and Lolita's mother, the tree means more than a mere piece of wood to turn into ashes.

There is only one way to honor this tree's life, Carmen's mother thought -- have it carved as a Santo Niño statue.

Catalina knew a man in Cebu known for his exquisite carving skills. He was famed for being one of the best carvers of wooden images of saints in Cebu. Without a second thought Carmen's mother knew she was going to have the santol tree carved into however many statues of the Santo Niño would be possible.

The sculptor's name was Teodoro Bentain (now deceased). His workshop was at Bulacao, Talisay (still is, now run by his children), just a short jeepney ride south of Cebu City. After Teodoro saw the cut santol trunk, he told Catalina that he could probably make two big Santo Niño statues and several smaller ones. That pleased very much that religious woman's sense of respect for God's living things. Eager to see how far the work was going, Catalina would visit Teodoro's shop almost daily, watching with awe and joy as the wood was turning into the solid personification of the Santo Niño.

Finally, after a few months, two big and several smaller life-like images of the Santo Niño, on their golden pedestals, were presented before Catalina. From the start the two big Santo Niño images were specially made for daughters Carmen and Lolita who were in America doing their medical specialties.

In one of their return trips from Cebu sometime in 1991, Lolita and her husband Celio, also a Cebuano and a physician, hand-carried on the plane the two big Santo Niño statues. Lolita and Celio live in Charleston, West Virginia while Carmen and Demosthenes live in Livingston, New Jersey. Before the two big Santo Niño statues were transported to the United States, before she died, Catalina had specifically asked her two daughters to inquire if the pastor in their respective churches would accept the Santo Niño statues to be placed in their church. The parish priest in Lolita's church in Charleston, West Virginia initially refused saying that he could not do it because then every ethnic group in the parish would ask to install a religious statue of their own devotion. After a few years, the pastor in Charleston, West Virginia finally consented to place Lolita's Santo Niño statue in her parish church when it became a Basilica Minore.

Meanwhile, in Livingstone, New Jersey, Carmen was refused by her pastor the same way, with almost identical words, with the additional "besides the church has already a statue of the Infant Jesus of Prague." When Demosthenes' sister in Florida became very ill, he and Carmen started coming often, eventually buying a house in Terra Ceia. One of the prized possessions Carmen brought down for their Florida house was her Santo Niño statue. Although Carmen remembers her mother saying, "Always keep a Santo Niño in the house to protect you," she also remembers her saying "Don't confine the Santo Niño. He likes to wander."

Through the years, Cebuanos are familiar with the countless stories from the caretakers of the Santo Niño at the Basilica, about their finding mud and grass stains on the shoes and vestments of the statue. It inevitably leads to whispered speculations that at certain times of the day or night, when nobody is watching, the Santo Niño wanders.

∿

In late 2009, when the building of the Santo Niño Shrine was becoming a reality, discussions began on where to get a Santo Niño statue to install at the Shrine. Several sources were explored. Cherry and Rene Bondoc, members of the Shrine Building Committee, mentioned that they had heard Carmen Co wishing for a way that she could carry her mother's wish to have the statue placed in some church to help spread the Santo Niño Devotion. At that time the other Santo Niño statue was already installed at the Basilica Minore in Charleston, West Virginia. Some members of the Building Committee also remembered seeing the Cos' statue in their Florida home. When Carmen and Demosthenes were approached, their joy was immeasurable. Finally, their Santo Niño statue had found a home.

And that is how the January 1990 celebration of the first organized Santo Niño Fiesta at Kate Jackson Park and the November 1990 santol tree destruction blessfully blended into one joyful event on the late afternoon of July 10, 2010 when Bishop Robert Lynch blessed the Shrine and installed the Santo Niño statue.

∿

6

Imprints

Virac, Catanduanes. Bonifacio, Misamis Occidental. Pontevedra, Negros Occidental. Talibon, Bohol. Parang, Cotabato. Maasin, Leyte. Oas, Albay. Dipolog, Misamis Occidental. Loay, Bohol. Palompon, Leyte. Pardo, Cebu. Manhuyod, Negros Oriental. Sudlon, Cebu. Tanjay, Negros Oriental. Inabanga, Bohol. Barili, Cebu. Matag-ob, Leyte. Marihatag, Surigao del Sur. Carcar, Cebu. Miagao, Iloilo. Baguio City, Manila, Cebu City, Cagayan de Oro . . .

All "faraway places with strange sounding names", like the song says. We were born, we grew up in those places. But we did not stay. We stayed long enough to know how to pronounce its names. Long enough to know the warmth of afternoons, the aroma of evening-blooming flowers and the church bells and meals of Sundays.

We did not leave those birth-places as empty, unfeeling vessels. We began our journeys carrying a deepening fondness for what shaped us in those places. We brought with us packets of memories. Our journeys took us to towns and cities in Canada, United States, Europe, Australia and other places with equally "strange sounding names," places we knew before only as dots on textbook maps.

We are now the round-the-world voyagers, like the adventurers who "discovered" us a few centuries ago. The restlessness of our "discoverers" have affected us like an Old World contagion. The awareness that there are other places beyond our hometowns prompted us to see "what's out there". Initially, simple curiosity, the itch of adventure, made us cross oceans casually. We turned into a journeying people. In the past twenty years however, leaving the Philippines has become a necessity rather than satisfying a curiosity of what is around the bend. Leaving is now an act of survival, the pure, simple, basic desire to seek a better life. Eventually, where our journeys took us, we learned new ways to live. But we did not cast away our old ways of Belief, of keeping Faith.

∾

To our new homes we brought the multi-shaded selves we had absorbed in the Philippines. For instance, our consciousness of people's social status, our special hierarchical attitudes towards the rich, the poor, the in-between. This thinking influences whom we choose to be closed to, who we welcome in our group, how we organize or disorganize. Unfortunately, it also influences who we want to pray with.

Then there are the many shaping tools and yardsticks with which we structure our lives – What status in life do we strive for? What must we have? What can we not do without? What human traits do we admire, what do we loathe? What kind of people we want to be closed to or keep a good distance from? How do we see ourselves in this new culture? In all of those, we are as varied as the shapes, colors and taste of Philippine fruits.

The Santo Niño Devotional group was not spared those interpersonal shortcomings. Any organization made up of people from varied life experiences, from different social levels and expectations, is bound to undergo such growing pains. But the Devotion lived through all those human deficiencies. It survived with non-disabling injuries, non-disfiguring scars.

Looking at our very different ways, our tendency to break apart before we get fully whole, we cannot help but ask -- What kept the Santo Niño Devotion intact, if occasionally bruised? Has the desire to pray together become the strong bond? Or have we been blest despite ourselves?

∾

In addition to the Santo Niño replicas most of us carry in our journeys, we also carry images deep inside us which will remain to our dying day. There is that one last freeze-frame of a face, a room, a movement that was the very last thing you saw as you turned your back on the Philippines. Our hearts "took" that picture at the last second before we closed the doors to our Philippine homes.

That final image can be anything -- the face of a sweetheart, a husband, a wife, a child, parents, loved ones left behind; the room where we grew up; the schoolyard; the street-corner where we learned immutable truths, where life had been revealed in all its glory or its harsh reality; the roadside snack bar and drinking corner; the riverside tree where we found love or got our hearts broken for the first time.

But one thing most of us did before leaving the Philippines – we went to pray for a few minutes in our hometown church. We went into that quiet dim corner where long ago we learned the simple outlines of sin and the intricacies of redemption.

That is a common last image of ourselves – spending our last minutes in that private corner where the echoes of every prayer we have ever said, every secret we have ever sealed, reverberate.

When we were innocent and malleable as clay, believing in the sensibility of prayer was one of the many imprints stamped on us. This is the one imprint from home that we keep trying not to efface, if only to keep us together and steadily in touch with our better nature.

7

Sowing the Seeds

Through the prism of the other imprints we bear, we get to know each other, we get to have a closer look at ourselves. Emerging through the haze and metronome of years, we see our faces, all of us survivors of the limits imposed by the relentless passing of hours. Cellular beings that we are, there is also our continuing awareness of our unspecified biological expiration date. It's a cognition we try to temper with our attachment to the sacred.

We try to keep our desire to pray timeless, not marked in minutes and dates. That is how the original participants remember how the group prayers began at Ledy Colina's house in Plant City -- vague dates, not formally organized, spontaneous and free-flowing. What is also widely remembered is the togetherness at the Colinas' living room, everyone fitting into whatever space was available to say prayers to the Santo Niño.

These prayers were routinely said with Ledy's family wherever they lived, whether in Beckley, West Virginia, in Philadelphia, or in Salisbury, North Carolina. Later, Ledy and Ernesto's three daughters, in their early teens, were actively involved. This time in Florida, in the late 1980s, it was being shared with whoever was interested among Ledy's friends.

For Ledy, group prayer is a family tradition absorbed in childhood in Carcar, Cebu. It was a tradition which was not just words monotonously repeated and absentmindedly heard but an on-going atmosphere, like the air the whole family breathed. The prayer recitations were interwoven with the daily sounds around Ledy, the tint and tone of her early self-awareness.

Sometime in 1987 Ledy, Ernesto and their three daughters moved to Florida from North Carolina. They settled in that Plant City ranch house surrounded by sentries of giant Florida oaks. The house was in the midst of a grove of sweet navel oranges which quickly became treats for the novena participants. As had become a routine for Ledy when they settle on a new place, she started her regular devotional prayers to the Child Jesus starting with just her family. She casually mentioned these prayers to her Filipino co-workers and friends. A few were interested and they started coming to her Plant City residence. It did not take long for those who initially attended to start bringing in their friends. Soon, a chain reaction took place and a good-sized crowd was regularly coming. Some were even driving from places outside the Tampa or Plant City neighborhoods.

The small prayer group quickly evolved into a spontaneous gathering of friends and other Filipinos, all with an unspoken yearning to recapture a concept of home. The prayer group was never formally promoted. It was purely one interested person telling another interested person that prayers to the Child Jesus were held at Ledy's place and everyone was welcome. "It was like a magnet," Ledy remembers, attracting many people she had never met before.

Soon, the participants were not just Cebuanos. People from other Philippine provinces, whose interest was mainly to pray together, began coming regularly. Even with the group becoming larger, there was not any thought to turn it into a formal organization. The informality, the spontaneity, the warmth of praying together, the new and old friendships, were all that mattered. Nobody imagined that that small devotional seed sown would grow into the Santo Niño Devotion of today.

Yielding to the usual human instinct to crown any organized gathering with a festivity, sometime in December 1988, the group talked about doing a "mini-fiesta" of sorts. It was planned to coincide with the traditional Santo Niño Fiesta in Cebu on the third Sunday of January. The result was the celebration that took place at the Colina residence on that designated date in January 1989. On the grounds of that ranch house, in the middle of that lush orange grove heavy with ripening fruit, shaded by towering Florida oaks, the regular attendees of the night prayers came with their home-cooked specialties. That spontaneous, jubilant feast was as informal as any gathering of family and friends. It is now retrospectively seen as the first Santo Niño Fiesta celebration.

The mood was of a family gathering, like a reunion-picnic of siblings and cousins who rarely see each other. Little did anyone know that this spiritual get-together would be the birth of a relationship among a diverse group of individuals. This proved to be the initial shaping block where the pieces took shape to become the Santo Niño Devotion of Tampa Bay.

Even then a sense of Family was already strongly felt, a sense that has prevailed to the First Friday prayers and fellowships. Through the years, it has been more acutely felt during the sharing of sad personal events and the joyous times of weddings, anniversaries and births.

After the prayers and the dining were over on that day in January 1989, the celebrants treated themselves to the pomelos, the sweet navel oranges, the sugar cane and assorted Philippine vegetables in Ledy and Ernesto's sprawling garden. Not only were seeds of heavenly graces sown that day, a harvest from the earth's bounty was also fully savored .

Spontaneous developments soon fell into place. The prayer attendees increased leading to the prayers becoming formally organized.

∾

Ledy Alesna Colina is a physician, a pathologist, who came to the United States in 1967. She was introduced to America via the Appalachian culture of West Virginia. Initially residing and medically training in Huntington, West Virginia, a town along the Ohio River, she later moved her training to the airy mountains of Beckley, West Virginia.

She was brought up in a traditionally Catholic Philippine culture which, in the late 1960s, was still inherently intolerant and even unreasonably hostile to non-Catholics. The religious orientation of West Virginia is rigidly Baptist and Fundamentalist, with patches of Pentecostal. It is often referred to as the "buckle of the Bible Belt". Ledy had to recalibrate quickly her Philippine Catholic rigidities to the explicitly Fundamentalist Christian beliefs of her patients and co-workers. It was a quick learning experience, a crush course in tolerance and understanding. These were crucial steps needed for her to face and accept as an emigrant. She has transported herself to a different world. In addition to her exposure to a non-Catholic religious environment, there was the compensation of being exposed to a distinctly rich and colorful Appalachian culture.

In Huntington, there were non-Catholic churches in every street corner. They were immaculately white in summer and picturesquely snow-covered in winter. They were the real life manifestations of what she used to see only in American-made Christmas cards. On Sundays, on her way to Mass, Protestant hymns resound from the car radio, Ledy's musical accompaniment.

Part of Ledy's childhood was spent around the hustle and bustle of her mother's restaurant in Carcar, Cebu. It was a childhood suffused daily with the multiflavored aromas from the kitchen. It was a busy restaurant on the town rotunda, a favorite lunch and dinner stop for buses traversing between Cebu City and the southernmost tip of Cebu Island.

Her earliest exposure to the Child Jesus Devotion took place during the months of her childhood spent at her grandfather's farm. This maternal grandfather was the patriarch of the family and also of the farm workers. Like a town with the church in the center, he had a chapel built in the central part of the farm. The wooden structure, roofed with galvanized iron, was surrounded by an expanse of tobacco crops and rows of coconut trees.

Even when she was still very young, this grandfather would tell Ledy that the Devotion to the Child Jesus was a family tradition carried through generations. Sticking to this family tradition, her grandfather, his family and his farm-workers marked every 3rd Sunday of every month with prayers followed by everyone dining in the middle of the farm. Then, on every Feast of the Santo Niño in January, her grandfather had the farm tenants do the novena, simultaneous with the novena in Cebu City at the San Agustin Church, now the Basilica.

Each night of the novena week, specific groups among the farm workers were assigned to put together a simple celebration after the prayers – a dance, an amateur singing contest or traditional feasting among the farm families. At the eve of the fiesta, her grandfather would bring an out-of-town drama troupe to stage a three-hour play dramatizing tales of countryside romance and other fables of broken and mended hearts. The Fiesta itself would start with a Mass, followed by feasting, all attended by friends and Santo Niño devotees from neighboring barrios.

Ledy's mother, the daughter of that Grand Old Man, picked up this Devotion to the Child Jesus early on. She expanded her father's original idea, building a chapel not only in one farm, but in every farm she and Ledy's father had. No matter how small the piece of land was, if enough families lived there, Ledy's mother had a chapel built. And she saw to it that every January, prayers to the Santo Niño were held.

In 1976, Ledy's parents visited her and her family in Philadelphia where she and Ernesto had their medical practice. Occupying a special place in her mother's luggage was a statue of the Child Jesus. It was a gift for Ledy, for her to continue the family Devotions she grew up with. Then her mother added – "It was also to keep us safe in this long journey". That particular Santo Niño statue occupies a special niche in Ledy's house today.

Carrying a replica of the Santo Niño when one travels, as Ledy's mother did, is a common thing for Filipinos. The statue or image of the Santo Niño is an indispensable item when Filipinos travel as are the snacks (*bawon, baon*) lest they get stranded in some desolate place. The Santo Niño is to feed the soul, and the snacks, well, you know. My own grandmother, every time she did the two-hour, sixty-kilometer trip to Cebu City on the bus, never failed to wrap in her *panuelo* three hard-boiled eggs, a few crackers and a small printed image of the Santo Niño neatly wrapped in cellophane. Of course, before she would do anything, her first stop in the city was to visit San Agustin Church, the home of the Santo Niño.

Ledy has continued her closeness and dedication to the Santo Niño Devotion. She was an active member of the Shrine Building Committee and the present Vice-President of the Santo Niño Organization. Most of the individuals who used to pray at her house in 1988 continue to be the strong backbone of the Santo Niño Organization. Her praying group has not only found a home, they have created in the Santo Niño Devotion a Family.

8

A Devotion Comes in from the Cold

There are as many reasons to move down to Florida as there are varieties of flora and fauna in the Everglades. Having found better jobs and opportunities. Advancing years. Retirement and a real love for fishing. An insatiable desire to dine on peppery, rich Hispanic cooking. An increasing abhorrence for driving on icy roads. The list seems endless.

For Filipinos however, it is still first and foremost, the desire to be in a warm climate. A Filipino's body thermostat, sooner or later, breaks down with excessive exposure to arctic winds and reverts to its basic need for tropical breezes.

For Max Montayre, (now Deacon Max), and his wife Concepcion, known to everyone as 'Chit', it was the realization that they were already often by themselves in their Chicago home. Their sons were in school or on their own. In their absence, Max was increasingly doing the necessary winter chores, especially shoveling snow. He was increasingly aware that his physical agility was receding as fast as his hairline. Besides, Chit, always the mother, wanted to live near their son stationed at MacDill Air Force Base in Tampa. In the end no other reason was stronger than the mother's wishes. Consequently, they moved to Tampa in 1984.

Concepcion 'Chit' Pacaña Montayre is a city girl, raised in the booming, post-WWII Cebu City, a product of Catholic schools from childhood to her graduation from the University of San Carlos with a Business Administration degree. She grew up in a household constantly filled with the sounds and images of prayer and devotion. As far she can remember, her mother was always close to the activities of San Agustin church, where the original Santo Niño is installed.

After every Fiesta in January, the caretakers of the Santo Niño at the San Agustin church has a ritual – the changing of the statue's garments from the festive ones worn for the Fiesta to the garments for the daily exposure to the people the rest of the year. Sometimes when the statue gets new garments, the old ones are given away to chosen devotees like a relic. In one of those years after the changing of the garments, Chit's mother was given a Santo Niño undergarment. This was a prized religious possession for her mother, the undergarment placed on a special corner of the home altar.

Chit and her three sisters, were devotees of Our Lady of Lourdes all their lives. For every religious activity they went to, they wore the white dress with the light blue sash. Chit continued this devotion until she got married.

Max grew up in a barrio in Barili town, (now Barangay Mantayupan). It is a lushly green community, sitting on top of a layer of mountains, overlooking a waterfall, Mantayupan Falls. Barili is a town in the southwest shore of Cebu Island, sixty kilometers from Cebu City. Max's visits to his cousins, aunts and uncles in the town proper entailed walking through mountainous paths carved on the side of hills. During dry season, when the mountain trails were parched, it took at least an hour to get to town. During the rainy season, those paths were dangerously slippery. Going to town was pure adventure.

Max's father was an agricultural school graduate. He used this expertise in his farming. The religious environment in his childhood was loose and casual. There was no church in his barrio and attending Mass on Sundays in the town needed that one-hour-plus walk through mountain paths. Masses were held only in the Barili town proper. Those frequent treks on the mountainside to attend Mass can now be seen as the metaphoric beginnings of Max's journey to grace.

Sometimes the routines of running a home and a farm kept the family from making the trip to church. There was also the heavy rains of the monsoon season which rendered the paths muddy and unpassable.

When Max and his siblings were older, their parents realized their need to go to Mass regularly on Sundays. Consequently, they were sent to town on Saturdays to stay with their cousins. This did not only assured their going to church Sunday mornings, this also started their exposure to four unmarried aunts whom Max described as "very religious." These aunts spent hours daily at the Barili parish church, from morning until late afternoon, doing various volunteered chores – decorating the altar, arranging flowers and candles, cleaning, teaching catechism, straightening out or fixing anything. Anyone living in Barili at that time can easily remember these four ladies, moving quietly all over the vast church expanse, unceasingly doing chores. Their names were also as familiar to the townspeople as the name of the parish priest.

These four *beatas* saw to it, strictly and meticulously, that their nieces and nephews, like Max, learn their prayers and observe faithfully religious activities and obligations. Max vividly remembers how he dreaded those days when he had to stay in these four aunts' house with the nightly recitation of the rosary and endless novenas. He attributes to those aunts' prayers his eventual decision to become a Deacon in 1994 as his dedication to the Santo Niño Devotion. The reality is that when he arrived in Chicago in 1969, already married to Chit, his religious observance was anything but fervent.

∽

Their first few years in Chicago were spent adjusting to life in America, raising their sons and earning a living. Nothing different from the early years of any emigrant. They attended Mass on Sundays but home and work activities took precedence daily. Church involvement was not a priority.

One Sunday Max saw in church an announcement of something called "a three-day Renewal". His curiosity aroused, he attended. This turned out to be an intensive Retreat. For three days he listened, and listened, and absorbed. It turned out to be Max's awakening, the dawning of an awareness that his religious observance badly needed a serious tune-up. He has never let up since then – becoming active in several devotions in Chicago including the Santo Niño Devotion, initiating the Devotion in Tampa and, eventually, the profound decision to get into the intensive studies leading to being ordained as a Deacon in June 1997.

∾

Typical of Filipino emigrants in their new homes seeking each other's company, Max and Chit were members of several Filipino groups in Chicago. In the late 1960s, early 1970s, the only place in America with more Filipinos than Chicago was the U.S. West Coast. As commonly seen in Filipino groups, as soon as it acquires a semblance of being organized, it infuses to itself a religious flavor. Praying together, being devotional to a particular Catholic icon, are soon part of its main activities.

In Chicago, after Max's religious awakening, he and Chit became active in the various religious activities going on. This led them to join a Cebuano Santo Niño Group which began as a circulating rosary prayers on weekends in designated family homes. In the beginning there was no regular Santo Niño novena. The first few Fiesta celebrations were held at the basement of a parish church as a casual get-together, opening with prayers to a Santo Niño statue which a member provided. Camaraderie and hearty sharing of each other's cooking naturally followed. In these Fiesta celebrations there was no procession because Chicago in January is not a place for outdoor activities irrespective of how religious.

By the time Max and Chit were leaving Chicago for Tampa in 1984, they have already been active participants in the various Chicago Santo Niño Devotion groups for five years. By that time, there were already many Santo Niño Devotion groups in the Chicago Filipino community. They left Chicago hoping that in Tampa they could join an on-going Santo Niño Devotion. When they got to Tampa there was the prayer group at Ledy Colina's which Max and Chit started attending.

∾

Max, in his years in America, had noticed that when Filipinos are together they either go fishing, have mahjong marathons, or eat and drink in endless cycles of birthdays and wedding anniversaries. When the Ang Bisaya organization was already on its firm footing,

Ledy Colina, Max and Ed Bilbao, already active members of that secular organization, started exploring the possibility of including a Santo Niño Devotion to the on-going Ang Bisaya activities. From those talks, the Santo Niño Devotion was began.

Since Max's ordination as Deacon of the Catholic Church, he is not only seen as one of the movers who got together the initial Santo Niño Devotion in Tampa but also as Deacon Max, a Spiritual Adviser of the organization. In all of the activities of the Devotion, 'Chit' is inevitably present doing all sorts of chores. Both she and Deacon Max are Founding Directors of the Santo Niño Devotion.

9

Patience and Perseverance Personified

After most of us have moved on to our Final Destination, some curious individual might ask for a human face with which to remember the Santo Niño Devotion. If fairness and sensibility still exist in that future time, this would be the answer – There were actually two faces and their names were Ed and Susan Bilbao. Today, it is safe to say that everyone, even those remotely involved with the Santo Niño Devotion know Ed and Susan.

When the Devotion was just a frail sprout in a seedling pot, Ed and Susan were there nurturing it. When the Devotion was putting down firmer roots on the grounds of St. Paul Church, Ed and Susan were there sustaining its growth. When the every-Friday Santo Niño prayers at St. Paul were sparsely attended by only the very faithful, Ed and Susan forged on. There were Fridays when it was just the two of them and two strangers wandering in who were doing the prayers. During those days in the mid-1990s, on late Friday afternoons, Ed and Susan could be seen at the St. Paul parking lot, carrying to church a small statue of the Santo Niño, a poignant image of persistence.

But blessed winds were blowing behind them – quietly, the support for the Santo Niño Devotion was continuing to increase. Soon, individuals who are still closely identified with the Devotion, joined with their unstinting support.

When the Devotion expanded, it was clearly seen as a result of Ed's and Susan's patience and perseverance .

∽

In 1983 Ed Bilbao arrived in Tampa straight from Cebu to work at the main office of an import-export company which had a branch in Cebu. This was the very first time he had been out of the Philippines. He had just recently married Susan who was left in Cebu. He did not know anyone in Tampa. Fully aware that the best way to meet Filipinos is to go to the nearest Catholic church, on his first Sunday in this unfamiliar place, he went to Incarnation Church. After the mass, Ed, being naturally sociable and adept at initiating conversation, introduced himself to some of the Filipinos he saw.

Thus began his friendship with the Filipinos in the Tampa Bay area. That initial meeting began a chain of acquaintances.

As is inevitable, mutually initiated social gatherings became regular. Ed saw that the Tampa Bay area was populated with Filipinos from a variety of social and professional backgrounds but with one common characteristic – they love regular get-togethers. There was a pervasive desire for a sense of home. Everyone was still adjusting to their uprooted state while simultaneously searching for the fertile ground to grow on.

Amidst the seemingly endless weekend drinking, dining and reminiscing about the Philippines, Ed and his friends started talking about forming an organization. Ed, mindful still of his Melchizedekian persuasion, initially thought of starting a Devotional Group, a prayer and reflection group. But he noted that the interests of the people in his usual company were of a more secular nature. Serious discussions began and from that was born the Ang Bisaya, an organization purely for nonreligious activities.

But Ed did not forget how important, even for secular groups, to have a religious framework behind its foundations. His earthbound practical sense has always been attached to a matrix of Faith and Belief. When the organizational framework of Ang Bisaya had firmed up, Ed discussed with Ledy Colina and Max Montayre, not yet a Deacon then, to explore the possibility of starting a Santo Niño Devotion within Ang Bisaya. This was an idea of course which had been brewing in Max's and Ledy's minds.

Ed grew up in Matag-ob, a barrio in Palompon, a town in north-western Leyte, facing northern Cebu. There was no Catholic church in that barrio. The only church was Protestant. Unintentionally starting his own personal pre-Vatican II Ecumenical Movement, the curious pre-teen Ed started going to that Protestant church for Bible studies. He developed this interest because he grew up listening to Bible stories from his paternal grandmother. A few years later, Father Miguel Logronio, a missionary Catholic priest, opened a Catholic church with San Antonio de Padua, (Saint Anthony), as its patron saint. San Antonio was the 13th century Franciscan monk who lived in Padua, Italy but was born in Portugal. He was known to be the saint to pray for to recover lost possessions and find missing persons. As emigrants, we sometimes feel that we have lost the earthly moorings we were once attached to. We also get the sense that people we have left behind have gone missing. By some stretch of metaphorical meanings, San Antonio might be the emigrant's ideal patron saint. For Ed as an emigrant, this might be the reason why the patron saint of the first Catholic church in his birthplace lingers in his memory.

Young Ed became quickly involved in the barrio's Catholic church activities such as Flores de Mayo. Even at that early age he was fascinated with all the church rituals – the Mass, consecration of the Host, baptism, blessings of any kind -- so much so that as soon as he was qualified, he started serving as an altar boy. Most of the time, he slept at the convent with the other altar boys so they would be ready for the early mass. By this time, the parish priest was Father Olidan, who became a very significant influence in Ed's life, being the very first person to ask him if he was interested in entering the seminary.

In 1963, Ed entered the seminary at the Archdiocese of Palo, a municipality literally in the opposite eastern coast from Palompon. To get there from Palompon, one has to cross the whole province of Leyte from west to east. Later, he continued his seminary studies at the University of Santo Tomas in Manila, then to San Carlos Seminary in Cebu.

In one of those situations which seem to foretell a person's future, one of Ed's early pastoral works was with the Santo Niño devotion at the Santo Niño de Tacloban church. Later, he was assigned to the Santo Niño de Cebu church in Isabel, Leyte. A path seemed to have been paved for him early on in the direction of a deeper involvement with the devotion of the Child Jesus.

The relationship with Susan went through many trying, stormy times because of his Melchizedekian status. Vehement and serious objections came from all quarters -- from Susan's family, especially her father, and from Ed's ecclesiastical superiors. How it was eventually resolved, leading to their marriage in 1982, can be seen through the lenses of what they had made of their union in the service of lay ministry. The fulfillment in their marriage, especially in their lay ministerial work, is a manifestation of what Ed calls "God's intention for all of us, the way He guides our different journeys to varied points of grace."

What keeps them going is their ever present awareness that from their initial difficult and unconventional beginning, they have forged a partnership which has paved not only their own spiritual path but also for many others. In addition to their steady, undeviating work for the Santo Niño Devotion are their many church lay activities for groups and individuals.

Ed was alone in Tampa for a year until Susan joined him in 1984. Initially, like most Filipinos who have never been anywhere outside their Philippine homes, Susan felt adrift in an unfamiliar culture. She thought she would never survive life in America. She wanted Ed to be always with her, being the only familiar thing in her life in those early days. With Ed at work, she kept checking the clock, counting the hours when Ed would be finally home. Even if she had already done household work in the Philippines, the demands of being the only person doing every single household duty felt exhausting. Many times she thought, "If this is what life in America is all about, I want to go home. I don't want any part of this."

Susan noticed that Ed was getting tired of her constantly discussing her discomforts, her loneliness for her family, so she started to mention it less. In the meantime, Ed was constantly reminding her that things would get better.

She constantly prayed for ways to adjust and cope with her new life. She sought new friendships which soon made her feel less lonely, less lost. Through the friendships that Ed had made, she met more Filipinos. Wherever she went at that time, she carried the small Santo Niño statue that she and Ed bought right after their wedding in Cebu.

Shortly after she joined Ed in Tampa, she learned the story about this particular Santo Niño statue. Flying to the United States in 1983, apprehensive about leaving the Philippines for the first time, Ed was holding this Santo Niño in his hand. Noticing the statue, the stewardess asked if it was a toy. In the next few seconds, Ed considered what would be the best response. A smart-alecky sarcastic answer implying the stewardess' ignorance? Unfair and rude, he thought. He was 30,000 feet airborne and the stewardess was obviously non-Catholic. A light, jokey comment? A serious religious explanation and a mini-lecture on the history of the Santo Niño Devotion in the Philippines? Definitely uncalled for, he thought. With a friendly smile Ed finally settled on the best response for that circumstance —"No, it's not a toy", after which he reclined into his trans-Pacific nap, the Santo Niño statue snugly reposed in his pocket.

To this day, Ed and Susan still have that Santo Niño statue, the "toy" Santo Niño, kept in their home in a very special place.

∾

After a month or two in Tampa, when Ed was at work, after doing the housework, Susan would walk to the nearest Catholic church. She would sit in the pews for long periods of time, sometimes alone in the whole church. It helped Susan's adjustment to America immensely that Catholic churches all over the world look and feel almost the same. Many were the times, sitting alone in a neighborhood Catholic church, when she would lose the moment and actually felt that she was back in a Cebu church. In those fleeting moments, she was home again. But even if her reverie was broken by non-Philippine sounds and voices, the familiar images and statues of the Blessed Virgin, the Crucified Christ, assorted saints, gave her some sort of reassurance that something of home came with her. That convinced her that an important part of her life had not been completely left behind.

The part of home that came with Susan, all of us have too. They are those indescribable feelings we had absorbed praying our way through life in the Philippines. Those countless hours, days and years of novenas and rosaries said at home, in churches, in school stay deep in us, like the fragrance of favorite blossoms or the face and voice of a loved person. Inside those neighborhood Catholic churches in Tampa, Susan replayed in her mind the images at San Agustin Church in Cebu City, at Pardo Parish Church in Pardo, Cebu and at the neighborhood chapel where she grew up. She started to feel that she and Ed had found their home.

∾

Susan Navarro Bilbao grew up in Kinasang-an, a section of Pardo, Cebu, a town that is the gateway to Cebu City. It is the hum that introduces the full-throated yell that is the city. People on passenger buses from the towns in southern Cebu, after drowsily travelling for hours, could start to inhale that special city aroma on passing Pardo town. For small-towners from Southern Cebu, Pardo is the introduction to big city excitement.

Susan, even if living on the threshold of a big city, had a small-town upbringing. She had a childhood, an adolescence and early adulthood totally revolving around church activity.

Most of Susan's growing up years was with an aunt who was very active in the activities of the Pardo Parish church and community chapel. When she was in 5th grade, she was already actively involved in the community's Blessed Mother devotions. At an early age, she helped raise funds for the church. (That probably explains why to this day she is quite adept in that activity for the Santo Niño Devotion). She cannot remember not being involved with church activities especially charity functions. She was the secretary of the parish church organization when still in high school, a position she held until she was in college.

Like most people who grew up in Cebu, not only was she exposed early to the Santo Niño Devotion, she also has a Santo Niño story to tell.

In their house was a big Santo Niño statue. Her father, a lawyer, an official for the Cebu City government, was a regular buyer of sweepstakes tickets (the Philippine version of the lotto). As is common with the majority of sweepstakes buyers, he rarely won. In one of those losing moments, Susan's father was furious at the Santo Niño for not granting his pleas to win. He harangued the statue from one end of the room to the other. When household quiet was restored, Susan was so afraid that her father's anger at the Santo Niño would bring a curse to her family. Late that night, when everybody was asleep, she quietly crept under the Santo Niño statue to ask forgiveness for her father.

Her involvement with church activities continued way into adulthood even when she was going to college, staying active in parish organizations, even becoming president for the Pardo Parish Legion of Mary. Activities for the church are so ingrained in her, which explains her tireless dedication, not only to the Santo Niño Devotion, but to many activities for St. Paul Parish.

∾

From the smallest Filipino Ministry activity at St. Paul, to the extensive planning programs for the annual Santo Niño Fiesta, in a matter of minutes, Susan can be seen with her folders and bunches of paper, walking fast with purposeful strides, looking simultaneously apprehensive and confident. She then approaches everyone, quietly going through the details of everyone's assignment for the coming activities. Susan does not only assign, she executes herself multiple functions. She solicits funds, she makes endless organizational phone calls, she does church announcements, she plays host to guests at her house (most of the time Philippine Catholic church dignitaries), and, she attends seemingly endless meetings. Now that the Santo Niño organization has became big and complex, Susan is regularly assisted by individuals who have been there from the early years of the Santo Niño Devotion and have faithfully stayed. Susan says that without these individuals, a large part of the activities for the Fiesta and throughout the year could not be done. These individuals have consistently given their intellectual and physical services to the Santo Niño Devotion that whenever Susan is complimented about her seemingly inexhaustible energy, she always says these individuals are "the inexhaustible energy."

In the early days of the Devotion, Susan was already starting her breathless pace. In one of the novena nights at a physician's house, she fainted from pure exhaustion. In a panic, Ed screamed "Is there a doctor in the house?" forgetting of course that not only were the husband-and-wife hosts for that night physicians but, at least, six regular prayer participants present were also physicians.

That night Susan needed a health intervention. Since 1990, Ed and Susan, together with those who have been steadfast Santo Niño Devotion supporters, have given intervention and sustenance to the health of the Santo Niño Devotion, taking it to its robust state today.

∽

10

Her Personally Chosen Road to Faith

Even if still in the womb, most Filipino children have their Catholicism in place, ready at their first earthly cry to be wrapped around them with their nursery blanket. The child's Catholicism is as inherent as his or her parental genes. Along with his ABCs, the Filipino child learns traditional Catholic beliefs. On the lap of grandmothers, the Catholic child is taught the basic prayers. In some quiet church corner catechismal instructions begin. The bloodlines of Catholic Belief fill up and start to flow.

Marilyn Neneng Navarro's childhood was not like that. She was born and raised to a different set of doctrines.

For all those familiar with Neneng Navarro's dedication to the Santo Niño Devotion, this is quite a surprise. Her attachment to the Devotion is doubtlessly that of someone with a traditional Catholic childhood.

Neneng does her tasks for the Santo Niño group, quietly, unobtrusively. She is rarely noticed. But she does some of the crucial chores that keep the organization running smoothly. For the January Fiestas, she organizes and coordinates the Sinulog dancers. She does the nitty-gritty steps to get the decorations ready. She serves at the buffet line on First Friday fellowships. She helps the clean-up after every organizational activity. She sits at meetings to formulate and sort out important decisions. She soothes occasional bruised feelings among members especially during the hectic days before the Fiesta. All that done quietly, without fanfare, without ceremony.

What she does for the Santo Niño organization is what she had always wanted to do – to be an active member of a peacefully ran devotional group. This is one of the important reasons she and her husband Alan Navarro, (Susan Bilbao's brother), decided to move to Tampa in 1998 even if both had good jobs in California.

When they first visited Ed and Susan in 1997, both saw the unity and cohesion of the Santo Niño Devotion members, what she calls "the maturity and closeness of the members." Neneng wanted to belong to that kind of grouping having experienced devotional groups in California whose members are what she calls always "bickering then splintering." It left her confused as to which splintered group one should join.

Neneng was born to a family who belonged to an exclusive, secretive group in Cebu called the Moncadistas. Their main enclave was in an isolated town, Sudlon, a few kilometers of difficult, circuitous roads from Cebu City. This group is a religious-social-civic movement. In Cebu the group was perceived as mysterious and secretive, generally seen by Cebuanos as a cult. Neneng's family was in it for years because the husband of a maternal aunt was one of the organization's leaders. Despite its mysteriousness, the Moncadistas are known as a peaceful group which just wants to take care of its members' basic needs.

Neneng is a highly thought-of member of the Santo Niño Family. For that alone, it is instructive for us to know the background of the group which played an important part in her youth, including her religious awakening. There is also the fact that the man who created this group, Hilario Camino Moncado, is a prominent figure of Philippine and Cebu mythology.

Moncado was born in 1898 when the Philippines was cutting away from Spain but about to go into guerrilla warfare against the Americans. In 1914, when he was 15 years old, he went to Hawaii to work with Filipino migrant workers in the sugar and pineapple fields. He moved to the U.S. mainland in the 1920s. Observing that the Filipino migrant workers in America spent their time and money on gambling, drinking and other vices, he organized in 1925 the Filipino Federation of America (FFA), a mutual-aid organization which, under his leadership, sought to instill cleaner living and higher moral values among the Filipino migrant workers. It also functioned like a union to give voice to the migrant workers. When his organization became big, spreading all over the U.S. West Coast and the Philippines, Moncado acquired a messianic reputation which he encouraged. He published a newspaper, wrote and published inspirational books and travelled back and forth between the U.S. and the Philippines frequently. He got elected to the Philippine Commonwealth Convention in 1934. At the eve of the Second World War, he organized in the Philippines something called the Filipino Crusaders World Army, with him as the Commanding General. Hence forth, he was addressed as General Moncado. He was reputed to be quite active in the Philippine guerrilla movement against the Japanese at the height of WWII. On the first election after the Philippine Independence, 1946, he ran for president against Manuel Roxas and Sergio Osmena, Sr. He lost but his organization in Cebu flourished.

Those of us who were Cebu adolescents in the 1950s are familiar with the word Moncadistas. The male Moncadistas wore their hair long, flowing to their backs, way past their shoulders, in an era when men wore crew cuts or closely trimmed, slicked-back, pomaded hair. They kept to themselves, looking ascetic and aloof. Rarely were they seen in downtown Cebu City.

We can see that the Moncadistas was not started by an ordinary man. Hilario Moncado, grandiose perhaps with all his educational and spiritual claims, but nonetheless a charismatic leader capable of organizing large groups of people. His original desire to get Filipino workers in America to lead better, moral lives was a noble cause. How it became a religion of sorts in the Philippines, mostly in Cebu, is a complicated story with scarce available details. At the very least, we can relate to the immigrant aspects of Hilario Moncado's story.

Part of his legacy was the semi-religious atmosphere Neneng was born to.

∽

Whatever religious observance Neneng was exposed to within the Moncadistas, she remembers vaguely now. She says she is not really sure what principles she and the other members of the Moncadista "Church" were asked to believe except to live upright, moral lives.

The prayers they were asked to memorize and say were in Latin. It was never translated and its meaning never explained. The word, or the letters INRI, she remembers as prominent in their Latin prayers. They could eat only chicken and vegetables. No pork or beef. There was a lot of singing in their service but Neneng does not remember any of the tunes or the words. What she remembers as amusing was that all the baptisms, weddings and funeral services were done in the local Catholic church. Somehow she knew the Hail Mary and the Our Father but cannot remember how she learned it. And her mother had an image of the Blessed Mother in their house that she would pray to regularly.

Most of the teaching of the organization came from the preaching during the service. They were mostly about the world ending soon and what signs to look for which would forecast this event. For a child, this was frightening and Neneng remembers feeling continuously horrified during the preaching sessions.

When she went to high school in Pardo, a town at the threshold of Cebu City, she started going to the Catholic church with her Catholic classmates. That was the very first time she entered a Catholic church. Pretty soon, fascinated by the peace and quiet inside the Catholic church, she started going regularly by herself. Then, with a friend, she started going to the Santo Niño Friday novenas at the San Agustin church, the present Basilica Minore de Santo Niño.

Initially she did not understand what the novena and the other prayers were all about even if she understood every word, the prayers being in Bisayan. She saw the sincerity and the devotion in the people attending. She felt the fervor and solemnity with which the prayers were said.

When she was in Manila to take the nursing board examinations, she was asked to lead the rosary at the dorm where she stayed. She was embarrassed because even if she knew the Hail Mary and the Our Father, she did not know the sequence in the rosary. She told the group honestly about her deficiency then proceeded to learn it from a friend. Having learned it, the rosary became her main prayer for success in the nursing boards and to this day she prays the rosary everyday. She also started going to the nearest church from their dorm to kneel from the door to the altar to pray.

When she went back to Cebu to wait for the board results, she became a regular devotee of the Friday Santo Niño Devotions, joining the long lines of people to kiss the Santo Niño image. She regularly danced the Sinulog during the January Fiestas. Every Wednesday she would go to the Redemptorist Church for the Perpetual Succour novena. She had found peace and fulfillment in the Catholic church.

By this time, she already considered herself a Catholic even if she knew she has not been baptized. While waiting for the Nursing Licensure results, she worked as a secretary for a relative in Asturias town, in the west coast of Cebu. Convinced now that she really wanted to be a Catholic, with her relative, she asked the parish priest for the steps she should take to become Catholic. After the necessary lessons, she was baptized a Catholic in the town of Asturias. Neneng became a Catholic at her own initiative. She calls that "a gift I gave myself."

∾

Neneng is third in a family of five siblings. When her parents learned she was already going to Catholic churches, her parents warned her -- "People who go to church will always have lots of problems because God will be testing them." She did not buy into that belief and quietly continued going to Mass and praying at Catholic churches. She knew that instead of problems, she was feeling a lot of peace through her churchgoing. Now, all members of her family, including her parents have become Catholic.

Neneng met Alan Navarro in 1982 when she was already a nurse. Since her parents were already working in Stockton, California, she joined them and worked in her nursing profession starting in 1989. In 1992 she went back to the Philippines to marry Alan. In 1995 she came back to the United States with Alan, moving eventually to Tampa in 1998 where she participated right away in all Santo Niño activities.

On August 10, 2000 a fateful event struck Neneng and Alan -- Alan suffered the stroke which has left him a quadriplegic. Understandably, Neneng gets emotional talking about this sudden turn in their lives especially the most trying months that followed.

Alan went into a deep coma. All the treating doctors told Neneng and the rest of Alan's family that his condition was hopeless, that he was "brain dead". Neneng could not think, became totally confused on what decision to make. She kept praying and talking to Susan, Alan's sister. Holding on to a strong faith that their prayers would be answered, she went with Susan to ask the doctors to continue the life supports for a longer time.

Neneng kept on seeing in her mind's eye the image of Lazarus in the Bible being brought back to life. Everyone in the family prayed continuously to the Santo Niño. Some days later, Neneng was at work when she was called to the hospital. When she got there she was told that Alan responded by blinking his eyes when asked to do so. Alan had come out of his coma.

The next six years were very difficult for Neneng. Alan needed 24-hour care, frequently going into respiratory crises. He had to be rushed to the hospital often. This very athletic man, a varsity basketball player in college, was now a quadriplegic. But Neneng and his family never gave up in their prayers. He was in three successive nursing homes. Neneng was rushing from work everyday to check if basic care at the nursing home was being done because she knew sometimes it was not done. These were months of pure physical and emotional struggle. Neneng had to keep focused on her hospital work by day, then, no matter how physically worn down she felt, she would rush to the nursing home to help in Alan's care. She would stay sometimes until late at night knowing that she had to wake up early to go to work.

When Alan came home in 2006, the hardship did not stop for Neneng because now his care was fully on her while continuing to work fulltime.

Then the trial for their malpractice suit.

For three very tense weeks in September 2006, the trial took place. Everyday in those three weeks, she and Susan drove before daylight to the courthouse in downtown Tampa. It was pure agony for Neneng because she was the principal witness. She was the singular, critical person to tell the court what damage Alan has sustained as a result of the medical negligence. Neneng has never been in any court in her life. She has not even attended a trial as a non-involved audience. The only trials she has "experienced" are those in the movies. Now she is in a trial where the critical decision depends on how she presents the facts of what happened to Alan.

When the suit was decided in their favor, Neneng and her family knew the Santo Niño had answered their prayers again. Now full care could be provided for Alan and his family.

It is common knowledge that from the malpractice award, the Bilbao-Navarro Family has donated considerable sums of money for many religious and non-religious charities including the bulk of the expense to build the Santo Niño Shrine. From the pain and sacrifices Neneng, Alan and their families have gone through, are still going through, they have quietly shared with the church what they were deservedly given.

It is not often that a group, like the Santo Niño Devotion, is blessed with the muted, unassuming presence and support of individuals who help because they see a basic need. This moment in time, in the life of the Santo Niño Devotion, there is Neneng and her family, one of the countless faces in the crowd, who extends this kind of helping hand. Here is this woman, who at a certain moment in her life, coming from a wholly different vantage point of belief, sought her own road to Damascus. Neneng personally chose her own road to faith.

11

An Assured Presence

Individuals get together for many reasons – to hunt and gather food, to build homes, to create a community, to start a revolution. In the case of the Santo Niño Devotion, it was, and still is, to pray. Eventually, being regularly together is not enough. The impulse to organize formally sets in. This can be from a desire to have a structure, a cohesion, a unified direction. Also, from the pragmatic view that the desire to pray together may not be strong enough a bond.

Groups when organized need a set of formally elected individuals with the responsibility to plan, set an agenda and make clear the group's objectives. Since the toddler days of the Santo Niño group, when its aims and goals were still developing, the names of Maria and Jose Raffiñan have been on the slate of officers, a recognition of this couple's patience and stamina to bear the tedium and occasional roughness of being in these positions. They have persevered with these responsibilities despite their demanding personal and professional activities. Both are physicians, Maria, an internist and Jose, a surgeon. They have stayed as dedicated and true to their professions as they have done for the Santo Niño Devotion.

Maria, in her last term as president of the Santo Niño organization, patiently presided over the numerous, lengthy meetings which painstakingly discussed the plans and final implementation of the construction of the Santo Niño Shrine. She presided from the very first meeting in December 2006 to December 2009 when groundbreaking was done, then all the way to July 2010, when the Blessing of the Shrine took place. She also continued to preside over the final meetings to plan the January 2011 Fiesta.

Most of the meetings to discuss the plans for the building of the Shrine usually lasted late into the night. This did not only go on for years but also encountered a number of bumps on the road. Steering these meetings into the successful building and completion of the Shrine is a clear illustration of Maria's patience and forbearance. She credits her endurance to the equally patient, consistently focused members of the Shrine Building Committee. This is an accomplishment that must not be taken for granted.

(A full account of the complex process which led to the successful building of the Santo Niño Shrine is in the later part of this book).

∾

Most members in the Devotion know Maria as Inday Maria or Doctor Maria, and Jose as Jun or Doctor Jun. Both grew up in Cebu City, raised by families with a devotion to the Santo Niño going through generations. For a number of years until her death, Jose's mother, Mrs. Jovita Raffiñan, was a regular in all the First Friday novenas. Maria's mother, Dymphna Causin, is from the Causins of Barili, a family closely connected with the Barili Catholic community, also for generations. This is a couple whose youth and adulthood were consistently shaped by the sights and sounds of the annual Santo Niño Fiesta celebration at the San Agustin Church in Cebu City. Jose's sisters, Charito and Josefina (Pining), were equally nurtured by their lifetime exposure to the Santo Niño celebrations in Cebu. Charito and Josefina are not only regular devotees but have consistently performed invaluable assignments for the Tampa Santo Niño Devotion since its early days.

When the Mosqueras, the Dompors, the Colinas, the Montayres, the Bilbaos, the Gadors are talked about as names almost synonymous with the Santo Niño Devotion in its early days, the names of Maria and Jose Raffiñan are right there too. Both were in that small group which began the Devotion, praying in alternating houses from night to night. Both were there when what started as social gatherings turned into spiritual togetherness. Both have, at various times, held officer positions in Ang Bisaya, the secular organization which initially had the Santo Niño Devotion under its organizational roof.

This couple's responsibilities grew with the Devotion and their involvement became deeper. To their joy and gratification, they saw that their children were growing up with the Devotion. The children entered their mid- and late-teen years with the Devotion consistently in the air inside their home. As a result the children became involved with small and big chores in preparation for the Fiestas. Maria and Jun remember with amusement how their children used to involve their girlfriends and boyfriends in whatever chores they were assigned to prepare for the Fiesta. Some of those girlfriends and boyfriends were non-Catholics who got a close look at this particular Catholic activity and exposed to this facet of Filipino culture. The other aspect that Jun and Maria found invaluable is the way closeness in their family was fostered with the children's involvement in the Santo Niño activities.

All these children are professionals now, in the medical and legal fields. A daughter, a lawyer, has recently been appointed as Associate Justice of the Superior Court for the District of Columbia. Maria and Jun were emphatic in saying that during their children's school years, all their prayers were pleas to the Santo Niño not only for the children's success in their personal and educational efforts but for their physical and spiritual safety. They see their children's success as answered prayers.

Maria feels very grateful to the members and officers of the Santo Niño organization, who sustained their dedication to the Santo Niño organization despite those times when interpersonal tensions and misunderstandings threatened to splinter the group. But most of all, she is moved by the camaraderie within the organization, which resulted in more devotees from all over Florida joining the Devotion.

She regrets the misunderstandings in the organization which broke up some close personal relationships for her and Jun. They feel reassured that the years have brought about substantial repairs to those past disruptions.

The most satisfaction both of them feel is in seeing how stable the Santo Niño Devotion has become. Maria appreciates the sustained efforts that are exerted by everyone, every year, to structure the logistics of celebrating the Fiesta, which both have been deeply involved in through the years. When they talk about the multiple pre-Fiesta preparations needed to be in place every year, they never fail to credit several people starting with Jose's sister, Charito, usually in-charge of coordinating the food ordering, preparation and serving. There is also Jose's other sister, Josefina ('Pining') who has been taking care of the altar flower decorations for the Fiesta High Mass. Then the now deceased couple, Elda and Bob Jones, who used to help decorate the Santo Niño *caro* for the procession. Elda used to sew the *caro* "skirt", while Bob monitored every year whatever repairs the *caro* needed. Bob also helped Jose organize the sequence of volunteers to carry the *caro* for the procession. Every year there are usually many volunteers to fill the *caro*-carrier rotation. Carrying the *caro* is a promised offering, another *sa-aran* (see Sinulog Section), a promised physical-prayer to raise and parade the image of the Santo Niño for all to see. This effort is either reparation and penance or gratitude for an answered prayer. (The *caro* is a platform or an actual wheeled vehicle to carry the statues of Jesus or saints for the procession).

Before St. Paul Church had the Pavilion, the serving of the Banquet for the Faithful on Fiesta Day was done under two big tents behind the church. The coordination of setting up the tents and dismantling it after the Fiesta was Jun's special assignment. The night before the Fiesta, right after the 9th night novena, Jun with Tito de la Cruz, Ebert Singco, Chuck Kuntz, Lito Reynes and their crew would go to the lawn behind St. Paul church, and, under the subdued lawn lights, put up the tents. Watching them set up the tents momentarily brought back childhood expectations that next day there would be clowns, trapeze flyers and tight-rope walkers. What was seen the next day was not the circus but organization members skillfully wielding deadly looking cleavers to chop the *lechon,* (whole pig roasted over a pit), while others were serving it as fast as they can to an endless throng of hungry guests. You could see in the background Jun trying his best to keep the food line from breaking up into uncontrollable directions.

Now with the Parish Pavilion, the major Fiesta assignment left for Jun is to hang the multicolored banners at the Family Center and to facilitate order during the procession. When Jun talks about these tasks, he always remembers the late Bob Jones who was always eager to be of help all the way to the Fiesta of 2010.

Maria and Jun have a deep personal attachment to the Santo Niño Devotion having been in it from its developing years. With Ed and Susan, Dolly and Ben, Fatima and Gerry, Romeo and Evelyn, and the many who quietly work behind the scenes, Maria and Jun have painstakingly shaped the organization to its present full-bodied expression. These days, with the Shrine Project fully realized, even if still involved with the activities of the organization, this couple has chosen to put their energies on other pursuits. At the end of 2010, they have chosen not to be active officers but be on the Board of Directors and Founding Directors. But attention must always be paid to Maria and Jun's forbearance in sustaining the vitality of the Santo Niño Devotion along with the efforts of many.

ⵥ

12

A Mother's Devotional Companion

Since the Devotion's beginning, many husband-and-wife teams have faithfully contributed a variety of support to sustain the growth and integrity of the Santo Niño Devotion. Couples have worked together on the day-to-day maintenance of the organization and on the plans for special celebrations. By this time, not only have most of the older marital pairs stayed, younger couples have joined.

Ben and Dolores Mosquera are an integral part of these husband-wife teams. Both have served as members and officers of Ang Bisaya and the Santo Niño Organization. Ben was the second president of the Santo Niño organization. It was during his presidency when the Santo Niño organization became incorporated on December 8, 1996, getting its official name Santo Niño Shrine USA, Inc.

Ben is the second of six siblings, a son of a traditional Cebu family whose devotion to the Santo Niño dates back to many years before WWII. The aura of the Santo Niño devotion pervades their household all throughout his early life. He says, "Growing up in Cebu, I was surrounded by Santo Niño devotees who brought the Holy Child's goodness and love to our home."

He grew up in the San Nicholas district in Cebu City, sharing a childhood and adolescence with another Santo Niño pioneering figure, Jose 'Jun' Raffiñan. Ben's mother, the late Dionisia Mosquera, was a daily church-goer, who started her day praying in front of the Santo Niño statue in their house. Once he asked her, "What do you pray for?" Ben never forgets her answer -- "To watch and guide my children to live better lives." Whatever good things have been bestowed on his life, Ben considers all that as answers to his mother's prayers.

Every Friday in his youth, Ben would walk with his mother from their San Nicholas home to what is now the Santo Niño

Basilica to attend the novena. Anybody familiar with Cebu City would know that that distance is quite a walk.

Just like any child who resents any intrusion into his playtime, he remembers the many instances when he went to those excursions grudgingly. Yet, when the Santo Niño Devotion was organizing in Tampa, Ben was one of the earliest to accept responsibility in promoting the Devotion. He realized then how deep those times with his mother had become a part of him. Memories of those times have become the prism through which he views his life. The dedication he and his wife Dolores have put into the Tampa Bay Santo Niño Devotion comes from what he had absorbed at those Friday devotions with his mother.

After Ben's graduation from medical school in 1962, he began working with the World Health Organization in a research for a more refined approach to the problem of tuberculosis in the Philippines. This was quite an admirable choice for a young medical graduate because tuberculosis is a major health problem in the Philippines. This involvement later took him to other parts of Asia such as Thailand, Hongkong, Malaysia and India. As a result he got a government scholarship to come to the United States in 1969.

His adjustment to America was in New York. His unease on being in a large city was comforted by finding a Filipino organization – Visminda. It was an organization of Filipinos from the Visayas and Mindanao, thus the use of three syllables from the names of these two areas in the Philippines. That New York organization had a Santo Niño group which became Ben's first involvement in this devotion in America. It was also his first experience in organizing a Santo Niño fiesta celebration. That experience proved very helpful when he had to do similar planning procedures in Tampa many, many times through the years. At that time in New York, he and Dolores were going through their medical specialty training.

Prompted by Philippine-like weather in Florida and finding a more convenient setting for their medical practice, Ben and

Dolores moved to Florida. Early in their marriage, the couple prayed fervently to the Santo Niño for a child. Five years later, Dolores became pregnant.

Five months into Dolores pregnancy, their boundless joy was threatened when she was in a very serious car accident. Ben was following her in another car when it happened. The shocking image of those first few seconds, with Ben watching Dolores' car being hit, still haunts him.

There was serious fear that the pregnancy could not be saved. But in the end there was great relief. Dolores was spared from serious residual injuries. The pregnancy was saved. All of those Ben and Dolly see as favors from Santo Niño plus skilled medical intervention.

Four months after the accident, on September 25, 1985 their daughter, Shari Theresa was born. "Faith, love and devotion have worked again in our lives," Ben says.

That daughter, Shari, now 26-year old, practically grew up in this Santo Niño environment. She has been a regular participant in the Friday prayers and Fiesta activities since she was in her teens. Regular Santo Niño attendees are quite familiar with her presence. Even when very young, she was quite noticeable as the ever-watchful person beside the late two elderly mothers of Ben and Dolores. When the Santo Niño Devotion was becoming regular in its Friday novenas and January festivities, Ben's late mother, Dionisia Mosquera, and Dolores' late mother, Julia Estrella, were regular participants.

The presence of family members from the older generation was always considered a blessing for the Santo Niño Devotion. Most of those individuals were lifetime Santo Niño devotees at the Santo Niño San Agustin church in Cebu and other places in the Philippines.

In his involvement with the Santo Niño Devotion, Ben is most proud of the time when he was the president and the membership increased through his efforts to reach out to other organizations. Among the Ang Bisaya and Santo Niño organization members, Ben is known for his skills in organizing galas and fund raisers. He always hopes that the present bond among the Santo Niño devotees will be sustained for a long, long time.

13

Ang Bisaya: The Crucible

The Tampa Bay citizens in the 1980s were getting less senior and getting more junior.

The new arrivals from other states were not exclusively retirees anymore. They were considerably younger, in their thirties and forties, some even in their late twenties. Most were in the midst of full-time careers. The couples were in the early years of their marriage, career or parenthood. With new arrivals from other states and Canada, the Filipino population in Hillsborough and Pinellas counties, and in the Orlando area, was increasing.

Unlike the Filipinos who moved down in previous years, most of the Filipinos settling down in the Tampa Bay area in the 1980s were not easing their way to retirement. They were people still carefully plotting out their lives and careers, adjusting to new jobs, new social standings. Some were even fresh arrivals from the Philippines and other countries. It was a chromatic collection of individuals, professions and social backgrounds. There were the Filipino-American military personnel of various stripes assigned to MacDill Airforce Base. One of those military physicians was Ireneo 'Beeboy' Racoma who, with his wife Helen, immediately became staunch supporters of the Santo Niño Devotion. There were also the Filipino wives and children of U. S. military personnel stationed at MacDill or retiring in Florida. These were Filipinos of a more recent generation, with a broader, fresher outlook than the ones who had moved to Florida in the 1960s and 1970s.

∽

At that time, even if already well-situated in America, the Filipinos' emotional, social and political consciousness was still strongly tuned to all the stratospheric signals from the Philippines. The reign of the Marcoses had just ended. The excitement over Cory Aquino was in full bloom. Filipinos were hopeful again about the Philippines. Those who have been in America since the 1950s and early 1960s were talking seriously about retiring in the Philippines.

The phrase "New Philippines" was tossed around in serious and casual conversations. Its meaning had different shadings depending on whose idealized expectation was layered over the emotional Aquino phenomenon.

It was in this atmosphere, within this growing Filipino community in the Tampa Bay area, that the organization Ang Bisaya was born.

Like any ethnic group, the Ang Bisaya organization was initially conceived in the minds of a few friends who casually meet on weekends over grilled delicacies and beer. In this type of get-togethers, after the rich conversational vapors of gossip and political insights have drifted away on the wings of ethanolic belches, the talk inevitably narrows down to a desire to organize. In rapid succession, in the blink of an eye – although by this time blinking has been considerably, chemically slowed down – names are nominated, election is calendared and by-laws drafted. Then everybody's picking gowns and tuxedos for the Officers Induction Ball.

The Ang Bisaya was not organized this fast. But close.

Ed Bilbao and a lawyer friend, and other regulars in their get-togethers initially thought of organizing. Later, the group was enlarged with other Visayans in the Tampa Bay area such as Maria and Jose Raffiñan, Ben and Dolores Mosquera, Fatima and Gerry Dompor, the late Maeng Dionaldo and his wife Tessie, Ledy and Ernesto Colina, Max and Chit Montayre, Romy and Evelyn Gador and a host of others who are not Visayans but shared the views and camaraderie of the Ang Bisaya members. These individuals are from different professions and social backgrounds. The main intention of the organization was to be in touch with Visayans in the Tampa Bay area.

∽

The word 'Visayan' refers to Filipinos who come from the Visayas, a geographical area in central Philippines made up of loosely scattered islands south of the northern land mass, Luzon, and north of Mindanao, the southern land mass. The major islands associated with the Visayas category are Panay, Samar, Leyte, Bohol, Cebu and Negros.

If we imagine the Philippines as one solid piece of land some millennia ago, like one big chocolate chip cookie, then see it dropped to a tile floor, breaking into pieces, then we have a crude conception of how the Visayan Islands must have formed. The breaking up could be from earthquakes or erupting volcanoes or both. The islands could also be the tips of huge mountains inundated by a drastic rising of the sea.

Visayan when spelled with a 'B' (Bisayan or Binisaya) refers to the language spoken by people who come from the Visayan Islands. Most of the initial organizers and members of Ang Bisaya are from this area with Bisayan as their language. Cebuano is a language, a Binisaya variation, spoken by people from Cebu, the island where Magellan in March 1521 gave the original Santo Niño statue to the island royalty. Other Visayan islands have their own slightly different versions of the Bisayan language.

The "*Ang*" in Ang Bisaya does not refer to a Chinese surname. It's a Filipino word, (common in most Filipino languages), which in English translates as the article "the". *Bisaya,* with an emphatic accent on the last syllable, means somebody from the Visayas, assumed to speak Bisayan or Binisaya. So Ang Bisaya was originally conceived as an organization of people from the Visayas or Binisaya-speaking.

No matter how much we have absorbed our new culture and language, there are times when sharing personal stories, memories and myths of growing up or living in Cebu are better expressed in the original language. Or when the tone, nuance and rhythm of the conversation can be told only in the native language. Usually jokes which lose the impact of its punchline when translated.

In the Ang Bisaya gatherings, conversing in Binisaya became a pleasant, exhilarating way to refresh the brain and the tongue with the old nuances. This desire to reminisce in the original language got the Visayans together, later joined by non-Visayans. The Ang Bisaya organization quickly became a gathering place for Filipinos from many parts of the Philippines.

❧

Being a purely secular organization, there were no plans to bring in any religious shading to the Ang Bisaya. The early activities were mostly around personal celebrations, birthdays, anniversaries, induction balls of officers, picnics, weekend group trips, Christmas season caroling, all with very temporal atmospherics.

Shortly after Max Montayre moved to Tampa, he met Ed Bilbao who invited him to join Ang Bisaya. Some of Max's old Chicago friends, now Tampa residents, were already with Ang Bisaya. Max, who rarely rejects a chance to be with other Filipinos, especially Visayans, joined Ang Bisaya with his wife Chit. In Chicago, where the only place without a Filipino organization is in the middle of Lake Michigan, Max was officer and member of several Filipino groups.

When Ledy and Ernesto joined Ang Bisaya, the other members learned that she had been holding prayers at her house throughout most of 1988. Max had been hoping to organize a Santo Niño novena group like he had in Chicago. He and other Ang Bisaya members then asked Ledy if her group can be started as a Santo Niño novena group. Most participants in Ledy's group were already members of Ang Bisaya. Some Ang Bisaya members objected, wanting to keep the organization non-religious.

Eventually the Ang Bisaya members accepted the Santo Niño Devotion as part of Ang Bisaya's regular activities, thereby increasing the membership. Some Bicolanos and Tagalogs joined even if they had regional organizations of their own. This was illustrative of a general desire to include prayer activities in socialization.

The prayer group having grown so much, there were nights when it could not be accommodated at Ledy's place. Members offered to hold the prayers in their homes. A rotational schedule was worked out as to where the devotees would go on designated nights.

The circulating prayers were alternately held at the homes of Maria and Jose Raffiñan, Romeo and Evelyn Gador, Ben and Dolores Mosquera, Gerry and Fatima Dompor and at the Colinas. That began the commuting on prayer nights between three Florida counties, Hillsborough, Pasco and Pinellas. To minimize the moving around, three or four houses were chosen for successive nights in specific areas. Nobody minded the occasional long drives, even on cold nights and coming from a long day at work. People now remember those prayer nights as the best way to end the day, giving them a renewal of strength and a refreshment of spirit. Others say there was a sense of joy and excitement on those nights, being with old and new friends. Hearty, benignly raucous conversations, laughter, and, of course, the sharing of home-cooked meals always followed the prayers. These days, everyone has fond memories of those nights.

Actually, even if quite unaware, they were laying down the strong foundations for what is now the Santo Niño Devotion.

～

Organizations are not abstract concepts. They are not cleanly drawn charts. They are people, made of and about people. And no matter how spiritual they want to appear, the ecosystem of people is the ecosystem of land, sea and air. It periodically gets stormy.

Diverse personalities, personal agendas and ambitions, untempered egos can turn into a combustible mixture. This happened when the Santo Niño Devotion was already carried loosely within the Ang Bisaya's organizational structure. Interpersonal conflicts threatened the Ang Bisaya's organizational structure. The members who cared about the fledgling Devotion feared about its integrity compromised by the problems of Ang Bisaya.

The closeness nurtured between individuals and families in those prayer nights kept the Santo Niño Devotion from falling apart. But there was something more. More than friendship, more than mutual need, more than a sense of shared identity that saved the organization. Something indefinable. Something in the hearts and souls of the members. Something that would sound flat, phony and insincere if put into words. Whatever is that nameless thing, we can only hope it will always be with the Santo Niño devotees.

～

In one of the meetings of Ang Bisaya in 1989, Max and Ed suggested celebrating a Santo Niño fiesta to coincide with the traditional

Santo Niño de Cebu fiesta in Cebu City. The suggestion elicited a lot of interest, prompting a lively discussion, then unanimously accepted.

Since celebration means dining, the discussion immediately shifted to how the meals for the attendees would be handled. Charging the attendees a minimum fee for the meals was a suggestion that was turned down. It was generally agreed that the offering of food for everyone is part of the worship, physical nourishment as the earthly form of shared spiritual nourishment.

And that was how it began, as it is still being done today -- the food served is free of charge, an offering for devotees from far and near.

A bigger place was needed to accommodate this now sizeable group. It could not be accommodated anymore in a private home. Max and Ed were given the assignment to look for such a place. Max was allotted $200 to rent a place. He found Kate Jackson Park, an enclosed, partly developed city park hidden around winding side streets off south Armenia. It is actually on Rome Avenue in the historic Hyde Park district of Tampa. Through some circumstance entirely unrelated to the Santo Niño Devotion, Max inadvertently stumbled into a situation which facilitated his getting the place free of charge. So the $200 was used to buy candles, flowers and other needs for the altar where the Mass would be celebrated.

The whole organizational force was mobilized into the planning of this Fiesta. Ed and Susan Bilbao, Romy and Evelyn Gador, Maria and Jose Raffinan, Ben and Dolly Mosquera, Ledy and Ernesto Colina, Max and Chit Montayre, Fatima and Gerry Dompor, Fatima's parents, the late Bart and Severita Regencia – all went into an exciting, planning mode. Gerry was the Ang Bisaya president at this time. Everyone was spending whatever hours they could snatch from their regular daily obligations to firm up all the plans for the celebration. From decoration to food preparation, everyone had specific assignments to carry out.

Max, already a member of the St. Paul parish, approached the late Father Fred Buckley if he would celebrate the Mass. Father Buckley's quick assent was felt by the members as the first ecclesiastical recognition that the Santo Niño Devotion is a genuine devotional group.

In the days leading to the first formally organized Fiesta, the nine-day novena was held at the homes of the Colinas, the Dompors, the Gadors, the Regencias, the Mosqueras, the Raffinans, the Gianans, the Camposanos and the Montayres.

In the meantime, everyone was involved in hectic preparations. The assignment of putting together the proper liturgy was given to Ed and Max. Both surreptitiously printed Santo Niño prayer pamphlets in their respective place of employment. They engaged in an activity which violated their company's policy prohibiting the use of office appliances for personal materials. Ed and Max put their employments at risk to provide the devotees with the proper Santo Niño prayer pamphlet. They felt like revolutionaries printing contraband propaganda. They were having a little taste of how the early Christians felt, doing their task in hiding. In the end they were able to print enough prayer booklets for the Fiesta attendees to share.

It is interesting that the steps shaped and implemented that time for the preparation and serving of the food are still followed these days, if perhaps in a more extensive and complex way. These days, most of the Santo Niño devotees who were there in 1990, and are still in the organization, do the same tasks. Maria and Jose Raffinan, Ben and Dolly Mosquera, Fatima and Gerry Dompor, Leddy Colina, Nilda de la Cruz, Charito Raffinan, and, in later years, Helen Racoma and Flor Alquizola have become identified through the years as the people behind the planning, structuring, soliciting and serving the banquet to guests numbering now in the thousands. With them are the many, many volunteers who arrange and help serve.

As of the last Fiesta, January 16, 2011, the food was still free, still financed with contributions. But discussions are ongoing now to make some changes because we have all become poorer.

That third Sunday in January 1990 had clear skies. Nature kept the Florida thermostat to its expected January cool. The winds mercifully did not stir the dust on the grounds of Kate Jackson Park. The surrounding Florida oaks and roughly trimmed hedges provided some shadowy coolness.

At noon, an hour before the scheduled start of the Mass, about 200 plus people from the Tampa Bay Filipino community started arriving. A number of men wore *barong* while some women were in modernized *terno* dresses. (*Barong* and *terno* are the traditional Filipino gala wear, usually finely embroidered on a delicately woven fiber material). The Florida mid-day sun was at its usual intensity. Most were carrying their personal Santo Niño statues. The Mass celebrated by Father Buckley with warm, intimate solemnity was held inside a plain, artless pavilion. At the end of the Mass, voices rose in excited mutual greetings, joyful faces eloquently expressed an unspoken sense that a fateful beginning had just happened. An important foothold had been reached in the common journey of these Filipinos. A devotional milestone established.

A simple, short procession followed immediately after the Mass. A small Santo Niño statue perched on a homemade *caro* put together by Ernie Colina, carried on the shoulders of devotees. Then the inevitable sharing of potluck dishes.

In the midst of the after-meal gaiety, people spontaneously started the Sinulog Dance, right there on the dusty grounds. The dancers waved single flower blooms picked from the altar decorations. Father Buckley, in his amusement, did not quite understand what the dance was about. It must have appeared to him as a strange, sudden eruption of exotic, repetitious dance moves, done to a pagan beat. It was then explained to him that this is a traditional prayer dance specifically for the Santo Niño. Impressed with the uniqueness of it, this kindly priest with a Pittsburgh background and breeding, was heard to remark "This is the first time I've seen prayer expressed as dance", at which point he joined the Sinulog Dance.

Around four in the afternoon, on that third Sunday in January 1990, as these Santo Niño devotees in Tampa Bay left Kate Jackson City Park with their empty pots, plates and assorted kitchen and dining wares, that earlier unquantifiable sense that something important had been started continued to be felt. It was accompanied with a strong, deep awareness that a responsibility has been given to keep this group's integrity intact.

∾

(Author's note: On my trip to Cebu City in April 2011 to get the background story of the Santo Niño statue now at the Shrine at St. Paul, I learned that the same sculptor, the late Teodoro Bentain of Bulacao, Talisay, Cebu, not only personally carved the Shrine's present statue -- donated by Demosthenes and Carmen Co -- out of a fallen *santol* tree, but also the smaller statue brought by Chit Montayre in 1990 used in that first procession at Kate Jackson Park.)

∾

14

A Critical Phone Call

Fatima and Gerry Dompor typify the husband-and-wife teams that held on to the responsibility of keeping the integrity of the Santo Niño Devotion strong. They were very much a part of the organizing group which made the 1990 Fiesta a significant beginning.

Their tireless contributions to the Devotion through the years range from being officers to the smallest routine job. Whether it's leading the prayers and making announcements on First Fridays and novena weeks, to overseeing the organization's funds and serving at the food line, to ordering and delivering paper plates, plastic utensils, napkins and other needed basics, Fatima and Gerry readily do whatever task is at hand. Both have even served as President. Fatima had two consecutive terms the last time she served. Gerry was one of the earliest presidents of Ang Bisaya before the Santo Niño Devotion was started. Lately, for several Fiestas he has organized the Offertory Dance and rehearsals. Fatima was the treasurer until 2010, a position she repeatedly held. In all those both have shown remarkable reliability.

Fatima is a pediatrician in full practice and Gerry does accounting work. Gerry is usually seen more in public than Fatima, who likes to work behind the scenes. Gerry's consistently foreground presence is due to his skills in soliciting volunteers to whatever activity the Devotion is putting together.

❧

Fatima was born and raised in Dipolog, Zamboanga del Norte, the 7th of nine siblings. Her parents were both in the medical field, her late father a physician and her late mother a nurse. During the early years of Ang Bisaya, Dr. Bart Regencia, her father, ('Doctor

Bart' to everyone), was an actively participating Senior Adviser to the Organization. This "elder statesman's" advisory skill was later extended to the Santo Niño Devotion when it began to be organized.

Both parents attended mass daily in their hometown and raised Fatima and her siblings on the virtues of kindness, decency and consideration towards everyone. Serious attention to education was heavily emphasized by her parents resulting in all the siblings becoming professionals. Fatima's sister, Mary Fe Camposano, a nurse, married to Percy Camposano, a physician, is also a very active working member of the Santo Niño Devotion since its early days. She is known to every one as 'Pipette'.

The first religious celebration Fatima remembers to have participated personally occurred when she was in the elementary school. One day her father casually told her that she would be sent to attend a big religious festivity in Cebu. She did not know what the festivity was all about. She was put on a plane from her hometown in Mindanao to join her mother in Cebu where she had been visiting relatives in her hometown, Bantayan, Cebu. That big celebration Fatima did not know anything about took place in Cebu in the mid-1960s. It was not just any routine celebration. It was the 4th Centennial of the Christianization of the Philippines. That momentous event turned out to be Fatima's first association with the Santo Niño Devotion. It was during the 4th Centennial Celebration when the San Agustin Church, where the original 1521 statue of the Santo Niño is enshrined, was elevated to be the Basilica Minore de Santo Niño de Cebu.

When she was in college in Cebu City, she started to be aware of the Santo Niño because her sister Pipette regularly attended the Friday prayers at the Basilica Minore de Santo Niño. Fatima's regular devotion was the Perpetual Succour novena at the Redemptorist Church every Wednesday, a devotion she continued when she was in medical school in Cebu City. Right after graduation from medical school in 1978, she came to the United States. She joined her parents who were already in the U.S., "Doctor Bart" working at a hospital in Marion, Virginia.

As if abrupt adjustment to life in America was not enough, Fatima faced the pressure and stress of getting into a medical residency training program. Seeing that it would be easier for her to find a residency program in New York City, her mother managed for her to stay with a close friend and classmate from nursing school. It was just Fatima and that lady in that apartment. When her mother's friend was at work, Fatima was left alone to fidget with mounting tension, waiting for a response from the many medical residency applications she had sent. The days to July 1, when residencies would start, were dwindling. Still, she had not heard from any of her applications. The suspense was unbearable. She did not know what to do with herself.

Five days to July 1, then four, then three, then just a day. Twenty-four hours. Still, the phone was not ringing.

In a room of the lady's apartment was a statue of the Santo Niño. Realizing that prayers were the only thing left for her to do, she spent her waiting days and hours imploring the Santo Niño to get her a medical residency.

On the morning of July 1, thinking that maybe the responses were lost in the mail, she thought of going personally to inquire at the New York hospitals where she sent her applications. She was about to close the door to leave the apartment when the phone rang. She rushed back in to answer it. Then and there she was told that she had been accepted and should go to that hospital to start her training. The hospital was just one subway stop away from where she was staying.

Since then Fatima has not forgotten how Santo Niño answered her prayer at a critical moment in her life and career. From that lonely tension-filled room in the middle of New York City in 1981, to several positions in the hierarchy of the Tampa Bay Santo Niño Organization, Fatima 'Babette' Dompor has never left the Santo Niño's side.

Gerry is a journalism graduate of the University of the Philippines. They have two children. Their son Jay, an architect, introduced Alberto Portela to the Santo Niño group planning the Santo Niño Shrine, resulting in Mr. Portela becoming the architect of the Shrine.

15

Sinulog: Prayer as Dance

The Sinulog, the prayer-dance that amazed and amused Father Fred Buckley at the Kate Jackson Park Fiesta, is more than a reflexive expression of a tradition. It is not as instinctive as singing Christmas carols when there is a chill in the air. Its deep cultural roots are not confined just to Filipino Catholics but can be traced to how humanity itself uses body movements to express thoughts and feelings.

The human way of expressing feelings, emotions, supplications, pleadings through dance probably preceded speech. When the emotion of prayer can only be expressed with movement, a dance like the Sinulog takes place, a wordless reaching out to God.

Very few aspects in our nature are more basic, universal, and, yes, natural than communicating with body movements. To the day when we become extinct, we will be using hand and arm gestures, head motions, facial expressions, bodily postures to signal feelings and thoughts we cannot express in words. And who can say that back there in humanity's foggy past, we were not looking for a more expressive language to get in touch with deities and other more sublime creatures. That must have been when hand and arm gestures were felt to be too common, too everyday, when the language of worship and supplication needed more elaborate moves. That must have been when we discovered the eloquence of the prayer dance.

People all over the world have age-old traditions of praying in dance – the rain dance of Native Americans, the whirling dervish in Turkey, to mention just two. When the human spirit brims over with feelings, the most fulfilling way to express it is through song and dance.

Like most ancient rituals, prayer as dance is deeply embedded in Filipino culture, a part of its genetic programming. There is a prayer dance for a good harvest, for mourning, for keeping misfortune away, for bestowing good graces, for the expression of love, for going to war. It is safe to assume then that when Filipinos were Christianized, they carried over their ancient pre-Christian dance-expressions to worship the Christian God.

The Sinulog maybe one of those carried over into Christian worship.

Many are the stories told on the origins and background of the Sinulog Dance. Some say that in King Humabon's time, whenever there was a death in the family, King Humabon himself would perform a dance very similar in movements to the Sinulog. It was done to the beating of drums to ask Bathala (God) to accept the soul of the departed. The prayer-dance was not limited to petitions for the dead to have a graceful exit. It was also done for thanksgiving for joyful or productive events such as the birth of a child, a bountiful harvest, a victory in battle. (King Humabon was the king of what is now Cebu when the Spaniards arrived in 1521).

❧

As described in Laurence Bergreen's book on Magellan's "Circumnavigation of the Globe", on that day when five hundred Cebu natives were baptized by Father Valderrama in the presence of Magellan, later that night, King Humabon's Queen and her retinue of forty women were also baptized. She was christened Juana after the mother of the Emperor of the Holy Roman Empire at that time. After her Christianization, she was given "a very beautiful wooden child Jesus".

Later, with the Child Jesus statue already in the Queen's household, a story goes that one of her court jesters became gravely ill. He had been in a coma for days. One day, the gravely ill court jester was awakened by a dancing, joyfully mischievous little boy who looked like the Santo Nino statue. The little boy's dance movements, the legend says, resemble the movements of the Sinulog. The jester followed the little boy around in his dance, circling the room many times. The little boy, before anyone noticed, disappeared. The court jester continued dancing by himself. When he stopped dancing, the court jester was fully recovered from his illness.

Another story goes that years after the statue of the Santo Nino was found in 1565 inside that fabled burning hut, the Spaniards, joined in by the natives of El Ciudad de Santisimo Nombre de Jesus, (the first name of Cebu City bestowed on 1594 by Fray Francisco de Ortega), would celebrate every joyful occasion with a procession of the Santo Niño, followed by dancing worshipers. And it is said that the dance resembled the Sinulog.

Since that spontaneous Sinulog dance at Kate Jackson Park, the devotees have carried on the Sinulog dance tradition every Fiesta in increasing numbers. In the past years, it has filled St. Paul's Family Center to elbow-grazing capacity. It is done in front of variedly-sized Santo Niño statue replicas lined up at the altar for the devotees to dance to. Together with Father Len Piotrowski, the Pastor of St. Paul, the Sinulog dance these past Fiesta celebrations have been participated in by an increasing number of non-Filipinos introduced to the dance and its background story.

For certain families this Fiesta Sinulog has become a tradition. Susan Bilbao recalls that for her late father, Antonio Navarro, the Sinulog dance was the crucial moment of his Fiesta attendance. He would dance until there were only a few dancers left. There was a year when some devotees staged a pageant within the Sinulog dance, recreating the Christianization of the Sugbu (Cebu) royal couple in 1521. Susan's father danced the role of the priest who baptized the royal couple.

In the Fiestas in the past few years, specially choreographed Sinulog dances were performed by groups, staged as part prayer-offering and part entertainment. There was a time when Ed Bilbao's mother, Remedios Bilbao, (to this day still a spark-plug of a lady in her eighties), and Susan's mother, the late Lucia Navarro, got several senior ladies doing the Sinulog as a special group for several successive Fiestas. They called themselves the Golden Girls. They made their own colorful costumes, some hand-stitching the costumes themselves.

Anyone who has lived in Cebu is familiar with the endless stream of people dancing the Sinulog in the plaza around the Santo Niño Basilica in Cebu City during the Santo Niño Fiesta. Men, women and children, together with the candle vendors, do the undulating, to-and-fro dance movements as one vast congregation. Inside the Church, Devotees from all over Cebu, the Visayas and Mindanao would occupy every inch of space to attend the continuous Masses. People come to Cebu City even days before the actual Fiesta. There is now a large quadrangle facing an altar and all masses are now held outdoors including the hourly masses every Friday.

Most regular devotees who come every year to Cebu City do so because of what is called "sa-aran." That is a Visayan word meaning "a promise". This implies that "a promise" has been made to the Santo Niño that in His fiesta the devotee will make the trip to the Santo Niño Basilica in Cebu to give thanks for some answered prayers. These acts of thanksgiving to the Santo Niño can be for anything seen as granted by the Child Jesus. It can be recovery from a serious illness, being spared from an impending misfortune or disaster, being successful in a task, arriving safe and sound from a long trip, anything really that was prayed for the Santo Niño to assist.

The fulfillment of the "sa-aran", the Thanksgiving Promise, is expressed in dancing the Sinulog, usually with that big dancing throng in front and outside the Basilica. The length of time for the "promise" to be fulfilled depends on the devotee. Most devotees vow to accomplish their "sa-aran" for as long as they live, or as long as they are physically able to be at every Santo Niño Fiesta and dance the Sinulog. Even on ordinary days throughout the year, it is not unusual to see individuals doing the Sinulog outside the Basilica, or inside, in front of the altar.

When the person who has made the "promise" cannot make it to the Basilica for whatever reason, a piece of clothing or some possession belonging to the favor-seeker is brought by a designated surrogate dancer who then travels to the Santo Niño Basilica. This designated dancer, when doing the Sinulog, then waves the clothing, or whatever material sent by the devotee, to the image of the Santo Niño while the dancer chants the name of the absent favor-seeker.

⁓

Then there are those who prefer to delegate their Sinulog dance even if they are there in person at the Basilica. This happens on ordinary days outside the Fiesta season or during the Fiesta itself. At all hours everyday there are hundreds of candle vendors, men and women, around the Basilica. These days they wear different, dazzlingly colorful uniforms everyday to indicate that they are the officially approved candle vendors.

The person who wants to delegate his Sinulog dance approaches a candle vendor, buys a candle, and asks the vendor to do the Sinulog dance for his special intention. As the candle vendor dances, the requesting person stands by the side, lips moving in silent prayer, completely still, leaving the dancing to the surrogate candle vendor.

There are instances also when the person delegating the dance just walks away after paying the candle-vendor, leaving the dancing and the articulation of the prayer to the surrogate candle-vendor. It is not known whether this person is saying his private supplications as he walks away. Here, the fulfillment of whatever was promised to the Santo Niño has been turned over to a paid-for anonymous surrogate.

Others who delegate the Sinulog dance to the candle vendors are individuals who see themselves as of a higher social class. They think it is unbecoming for someone of their social status to dance with a crowd of a widely varied social standing. Even in prayer, they do not want to be seen with those they consider the working class, the servant class, the faceless, the nameless, outsiders of their self-perceived social exclusivity.

This might be a shocking revelation to some but this is another real aspect in the cross section of the Filipino praying community. A simple reminder perhaps that even in praying some Filipinos apply the calibration of social hierarchy. Daily activities, including worship, viewed through a prism of cultural and social consciousness still do exist.

∽

These past many years, the Sinulog in Cebu City, this simple, spontaneous prayer-dance, has been turned into a massive, living-color video extravaganza. On the day of the Fiesta, thousands of intricately, colorfully costumed dancers perform Broadway-style choreographed dances in a designated stretch of the metropolitan avenue. This Mardi Gras-without-beads, without disrobings, goes on for hours. It is performed for endless, jostling crowds on the roadside and a grandstand of government officials and invited guests. The array of civil and religious dignitaries on the grandstand resemble a congregation of Politburo apparatchiks watching tanks and cannons passing by in a Moscow Mayday parade.

Even if the dances are supposed to re-enact, in various lavish styles and costumes, the gifting of the original Santo Niño statue to the queen of Cebu in 1521, the Sinulog in Cebu City has become a Vegas-style tourist show. This extravaganza illustrates that even in the way we pray, Filipinos soon get bored with quiet, austere ways. Sooner or later, our beliefs have to be dressed in a grand and elaborate style, our prayers chanted to the drumbeat and trumpet blare of the circus.

∽

16

Quiet Dependability

Those with arboreal imagination might see the Santo Niño Organization these days as a sturdy tree with spreading branches casting cool, comforting shades. But the Devotion was not picked from some Florida greenhouse fully grown. It had its struggling seedling days. It had its days when there was real fear that it would not thrive. But there were many who stood by to nurse that seedling. And they are still here today, still closely tending to the tree's health. In that ever-faithful group are Tito and Nilda de la Cruz.

This couple was in that small crowd going to Ledy's house for those "family prayers" in the late 1980s. They were there when those prayer-gatherings were moving around from house to house, travelling at night with the zeal of hunted Christians of old. They were there when the first formal Fiesta was celebrated at Kate Jackson Park.

Nilda and Tito, just like any emigrant, had to find more convenient ways to adjust to their new personal world. Both were raised in homes where group praying is not only central to family gatherings but crucial to staying together. Nilda knew that when Filipinos get together socially, praying inevitably follows. She finds that participating in those prayer activities is the most comfortable way to recapture a feeling of home. So when she heard of the prayers at Ledy's place from Susan and Ed, she and Tito did not hesitate to join. The next thing they knew, the group was becoming the Santo Niño prayer group.

When Tito and Nilda came to America in 1974, they were already familiar with the Santo Niño devotion in the Philippines. In their hometown of Virac, Catanduanes, they grew up next to a barrio called Santo Niño where the fiesta was regularly celebrated. So when the prayer group finally focussed on the Santo Niño Devotion, the sense of being home became more enhanced.

The first organized Fiesta Celebration at Kate Jackson Park -- the mass, the procession, the Filipino fiesta-style feasting – clinched it for Nilda and Tito. They could not believe this was happening in America. It felt so much like home again, like a fantasy come true, especially the camaraderie. It transported them to the fiesta celebrations of their childhood.

What's more, there was the Sinulog. Being a purely Cebuano ritual, the Sinulog was largely unknown in the Bicol provinces. Nilda and Tito can never forget their introduction to the Sinulog at Kate Jackson Park. They were struck by the soulfulness of a pure, simple dance expressing the sentiments of a prayer. Now every fiesta, Tito and Nilda look forward to that time in the afternoon when the Sinulog starts.

∽

As the organization grew and became more complex, Tito's and Nilda's organizational responsibilities grew with it. They are noted for being hard-workers behind the scenes, the kind of members who make things happen without fanfare or fuss. Their skill to distance themselves from the usual interpersonal, organizational friction has made them quite an asset to a growing organization.

Nilda, being a Certified Public Accountant, held various levels of responsibility on the financial side of the Santo Niño organization. She was the Auditor for many terms and is presently the Treasurer. She also has another, rather unique, semi-permanent job, dating back to when the Santo Niño Organization started the mass feeding of the devotees – Nilda coordinates the order of all chicken dishes. This assignment puzzles her because in her personal and professional life she has never had any close association with edible flying creatures.

This assignment is not as simple as it sounds. First she has to get all the names of those who will contribute a chicken dish. She then makes sure that there is enough for the anticipated attendees and that the chicken dishes are brought in at the exact designated time and place. It is indeed a job which requires a Certified Public Accountant's instincts for precision.

As a Marine Engineer, Tito has always had supervisory positions aboard ships in the Philippines and in the U.S. His special skills in organizing groups of people to do a job within a limited time has also made him the semi-permanent hands-on supervisor of whatever crew is hastily put together to do many preparations for the January Fiestas. He does this almost every year, alternating the chairmanship position with Chuck Kuntz, another long-term Santo Niño group member. Both have had this assignment since the Santo Niño Devotion got situated at St. Paul Church.

The job entails organizing and supervising the crew to set up the tents, (before the Parish Pavilion was built), for the banquet; setting up decorations which require climbing ladders while carrying heavy tools; taking out, moving and putting back furniture; and the cleaning after the banquet. After doing this for years, Tito says he is more than ready to set up convention halls. For Tito and Chuck this assignment carries a fancy title printed every year in the Fiesta Souvenir Program– Chairman, Environmental and Physical Services.

This assignment has become so ingrained in Tito and Chuck that in some years when they had other assignments, they went ahead and helped the Physical Services Committee. Tito and Chuck's roles in the Organization however are not limited to these brawny tasks. In meetings where important plans for the Santo Niño organization are decided upon, Tito and Nilda, and Chuck, are there too, their views being consistently sought after with regards to critical decisions affecting the Santo Niño organization's progress. Tito and Nilda are Founding Directors and Chuck Kunz is a Board Director.

What is instilled in childhood, especially in spiritual matters, becomes a genetic circuit board informing the directions of people's lives. In Tito's case, it is the way he and his siblings used to be awakened by his mother on Sundays at four in the morning to attend the first mass of the day. His mother assumed that if they are the only children in that early mass, no playmates, they would not be distracted. The would give the mass their full attention. But being children, Tito and his siblings slept through most of those masses. That four-in-the-morning sense of discipline though has stayed with him. If a child is to be pulled away from sleep at four in the morning, he realized as an adult, then praying and taking care of one's spiritual being must really be important. Tito did not say if he and Nilda go to four a.m. masses these days.

What influenced Nilda in her childhood was the vast collection of catechismal books which her aunt possessed. Like any child, what attracted Nilda initially were the pictures of saints and the various stages of Christ's life. Then she started to read the stories about the lives of saints and Christ's Passion. The stories became emotional experiences for her, giving her a sense of why people pray. Since then she always wants to go and join people praying.

This is how it began for Nilda and Tito — the desire to be a part of a prayer group. In the regular celebration of a culture and tradition, which they thought they had left behind, both have found a sense of belonging, a sense of home in the Santo Niño Devotion. But what both may not be aware of is that they themselves, like many others, are the ones who shaped the Devotion into a Home.

～

17

The Santo Niño Devotion Finds a Home

After the Kate Jackson Park celebration more and more people joined the Santo Niño Devotion. Through the efforts of Ang Bisaya officers and members Maria and Jose Raffinan, Ben and Dolores Mosquera, Babette and Gerry Dompor, Romy and Evelyn Gador, Ledy and Ernesto Colina, Ed and Susan Bilbao, Max and Chit Montayre, the Devotion flourished.

The members and officers soon realized that the Devotion needed a bigger place to hold the regular prayers and meetings. The group has become too big to meet in private homes.

Max and Chit, Ed and Susan and other Devotion members who were registered parishioners at St. Paul were recruited to talk to Father Austin Mullen, (now Monsignor Mullen), the Pastor of St. Paul at that time. They were to inquire if Father Mullen would consider allowing this prayer group to use a space in one of the parish's buildings for their group prayers. Before going to Father Mullen to present their formal request, Max and Ed discussed it with Father Fred Buckley, who by this time had become the group's unofficial Spiritual Director. They solicited Father Buckley's thoughts whether this was a reasonable idea and how receptive Father Mullen might be. Later, Father Buckley came back with the information that Father Mullen was willing to talk to the group.

On the day of the appointment, Max, Ed, Ledy and Ernesto, Maria and Jose, Dolly and Ben went to see Father Mullen. These individuals were the most appropriate to represent the Santo Niño Devotion because they had been there since the Devotion's inception.

In the ensuing conversation, since they kept saying "Santo Niño", Father Mullen initially thought it was a Hispanic devotion and they were a Hispanic group. They clarified it to be the Philippine version of the Holy Child Devotion popular in 16th-17th

Century Europe. They left with Father Mullen articles about the Santo Niño Devotion in the Philippines, specifically in Cebu, and the central role of the Santo Niño in the Christianization of the Philippines. After some consideration and logistical arrangements, the Santo Niño group was granted the use of the parish social hall on specifically designated periods.

As a sign of appreciation for this official approval, the Santo Niño group offered to participate in the annual Fall Park Carnival, a fund raiser for the St. Paul parish.

This was how the Filipino Santo Niño Devotion found its home at St. Paul church.

Soon enough the Santo Niño group members became big participants in that annual Fall Carnival. They had a booth selling grilled chicken and fried egg roll, the final cooking done right there at the Santo Niño booth on the St. Paul grounds. The marinating, pre-cooking of the chicken and wrapping of the egg rolls took place at the Colinas, (referred to as "wrap sessions"), with the Racomas and the Alquizolas. The final grilling and frying took place at the booth as the customers wait. Before the grilling, the chicken was precooked to insure health safety and richer flavor. Very quickly, the Santo Niño booth became one of the biggest earners for this St. Paul Parish annual fund raising.

The carnival was eventually discontinued in the mid-1990s when Mons. Neff became the pastor. It had become so big and popular, attended by huge crowds, that parish authorities became concerned with potential incidents that could turn into parish liabilities. The popular Santo Niño grilled-chicken-and-egg-roll depot was no more, closed with the carnival. But the social and working camaraderie created during those autumn days of the short-lived carnival years was another strong factor that bonded the Santo Niño group.

∽

The novena leading to the 1991 Fiesta was held at St. Paul Church for the first time as was the Fiesta celebration, the very first held on the grounds of the church. The late Father Fred Buckley, remembered always as the gentle and warmly accommodating person, became the official Mass celebrant for the First Friday Devotions, occasionally alternating with his brother, the late Father John Buckley. Both did this from 1991 to 2000 when they went into full retirement.

Father John went back to Pittsburgh, his and Father Fred's hometown, while Father Fred stayed in Tampa where he peacefully died on February 9, 2002. His unceasing attention to the Santo Niño devotees was fondly remembered during his memorial mass. These brothers' closeness continued to be celebrated even in the date of their deaths -- Father John died in Pittsburgh, also on February 9 two years later, 2004. Both are buried in Tampa.

On November 6, 2003 the Devotion acquired its "own, exclusive Spiritual Leader" when the first Filipino Parochial Vicar for St. Paul, Jose 'Father Joy' Colina, joined St. Paul Parish, straight from the Philippines. He would stay for seven and one half years, November 6, 2003 to June 30, 2011.

The Santo Niño Fiesta Mass in 1991 was held at the church's Social Hall. It continued to be a humble affair although with a much bigger participation than the Kate Jackson Park celebration the year before. Food provided through "pot luck" arrangement was served after the procession of a Santo Niño statue brought by Max and Chit, the same statue used at the procession at Kate Jackson Park in 1990. In the 1991 Fiesta, Filipinos from other parts of Florida started to attend, an attendance which through the years have multiplied many times over.

A joyous, festive socialization before and after the Sinulog shaped up very quickly. Children played all over the church grounds. Lively, excited conversations between friends who have not seen each other for years resounded all over the campus of St. Paul. The regular St. Paul parishioners, coming out from the regular Sunday Masses, wondered about this sudden, unfamiliar festivity of equally unfamiliar faces. All over the informal, lively groupings inside the social hall, outside on the benches and on the grounds, was a palpable atmosphere of pride, gratitude and joy. Filipino Santo Niño devotees have found a home.

At the end of that day, Ed and Susan, Maria and Jose, Max and Chit, Ledy, Fatima and Gerry, Ben and Dolly, Tito and Nilda and everyone who had given so much to build the Devotion to its 1991 stability, dared, for the first time, to dream of building a Shrine.

18

Sharing a Personal Lesson

One of the consistent pillars of the Santo Niño group through the years, Arturo Raxtie Auza, began my conversation with him with his memory of that first Fiesta celebrated at St. Paul church in 1991. He knew from the excitement and dedication shown that day that the Devotion was here to stay.

For Raxtie who, with his wife Nenen, started their participation in the Devotion shortly after it found a home at St. Paul, that development tightened the bond that started the group together.

"Knowing that the Devotion had a specific gathering place", Raxtie continued, "gave the devotees a sense of stability and uniformity, a more defined identity. As the number of devotees increased, it also gave those living in other parts of Florida, in other parts of the United States for that matter, a definite center. This Tampa group has become a motivation for people to revive their own personal Santo Niño Devotion. There is a sense of pilgrimage for people to be together at least once a year". Raxtie knows this personally because through the years he and his wife Nenen have brought friends from other parts of the states to attend the January Fiesta. Playing host to their out-of-state friends for the Fiesta has now become a family tradition. To this day there are two families from Miami, (where Raxtie and his family lived until 1990), who regularly come to attend and celebrate with them every January Fiesta. Lately, Raxtie and Nenen have observed that on every Fiesta, new out-of-town friends come, attending for the first time. Then they end up coming back to subsequent Fiestas.

When Raxtie joined the Santo Niño Devotion in 1990, the first thing he noticed was the closeness of the members to each other. He thought that was unusual for a young organization until he realized that these individuals started as a prayer group. When he was still active in the priestly ministry, Raxtie had observed that Filipinos do not worship individually. They worship more fervently as a community. He had observed more passion when many voices are raised together in prayer. Raxtie firmly believes that this kind of communal spirit made the Santo Niño Devotion flourished.

While still living in Miami, Raxtie and Nenen would make occasional trips to Tampa to visit friends. In one of those trips, Gerry Dompor, an old friend, classmate and fellow Boholano, took him to one of the early Ang Bisaya gatherings. The warmly sociable Raxtie instantly made friends with the Ang Bisaya members at that time, especially Ed and Susan. When he and Nenen finally moved to Tampa, he already had this set of friends and acquaintances.

As is usual with Filipinos when in a new place, the first thing they look for is the nearest Catholic church. Raxtie knew that when they start attending masses getting to know more Filipinos inevitably follows.

When they joined St. Paul parish, the Santo Niño Devotion was already regularly gathering there. They did not only join the parish, they also became active members of the Santo Niño Devotion.

Although there was no Santo Niño Devotion in Miami, Raxtie's family with Nenen's mother, (now, a most familiar figure in every Santo Niño gathering, fondly known by everyone in the community as Nang Inciang), regularly have family prayers. Where they come from in Bohol, there is no definite Santo Niño Devotion but a lot of devotions to various patron saints. The saint most celebrated and followed with universal devotion in Bohol is San Jose, the patron saint of Tagbilaran. San Jose, (St. Joseph), is considered to be the husband of Mary, the Virgin Mother of Jesus. Wherever Boholanos are located all over the world, if they cannot go home to Bohol for the San Jose fiesta celebration, a fiesta would be held where they are.

The Santo Niño Devotion however is not unknown or unattended in Bohol. It is widely celebrated in many smaller islands which are parts of the main Bohol island, especially those islands facing Cebu island. Those islands usually are inhabited by former Cebuanos. Nenen's father, who worked in Cebu, was a Santo Niño devotee most of his life.

The Ang Bisaya and the Santo Niño group at that time was perceived, and managed as one group even if it had two separate slates of officers. For Raxtie and everyone who joined, membership seemed automatically in both organizations. In the meanwhile, the population of Boholanos in the Tampa Bay area had multiplied. To this writer's observation, there was a span of several years in the 1990s, when a large number of active participants of both Ang Bisaya and the Santo Niño group were Boholanos. Raxtie, his family, and many other Boholanos were quite prominent and visible in many Santo Niño activities. Some of these were Emilio and Gwen Iyog, Lydia Caballo, Lito and Eden Dano, Jun and Emma Calotes, Butch Hossain, Roberto Hossain and family and many, many more. Romy and Evelyn Gador were active participants in the original Santo Niño prayer group who later based their Santo Niño Devotion involvement with the Boholanos. Then there is that retiring, reclusive figure named TQ Solis, a gifted musician and composer who also came in the early 1990s and organized an excellent choir which performed in at least one Fiesta High Mass.

Soon enough the Boholanos, if only by their sheer number, became closely involved with many regular Santo Niño activities. Contributing home-cooked food to be served for the monthly fellowships and for the main Fiesta; decorating the Family Center for the Fiesta Sinulog; carrying the caro in the procession; raising funds, making calls and running a variety of errands.

Towards the mid-1990s, the population of Boholanos in the Tampa Bay area remarkably increased. Something inherent in Boholanos was bound to happen.

There is a common belief among people from the Visayan Islands that if you get two or three Boholanos together, they will form an organization. This is a legendary but also proven belief. Boholanos, wherever they are in the world, are known to congregate quickly into a close, cohesive group. (There must be an ethnological thesis on that somewhere).

Soon enough the new crowd of Boholanos in Tampa did organize before anyone could say Dagohoy. (Quickly, ask a Boholano who Dagohoy is).

This was not really a surprise because Boholanos had already well-rooted organizations in the United States and Canada. In the Tampa Bay area the organization, Kaliwat Bol-Anon, was formed. The name means "Kindreds from Bohol". It was initially led by Lito Dano, who arrived in Tampa in 1994 with his wife Eden and family. They came from New York where they were active in a Boholano organization.

This development created some tension, a cycle of misunderstandings, ill feelings and disruptions of relationships within the Santo Niño and Ang Bisaya groups because the Kaliwat Bol-Anon was seen by a few individuals as created to undermine and weaken the Ang Bisaya and the Santo Niño groups. This was clearly seen later as an erroneous and plainly malicious impression.

When events like these occur, there are inevitably individuals who, for their own personal reasons, want to fuel the fire. There then ensued a span of time when personal and organizational relationships between significant individuals of Ang Bisaya and Kaliwat-Bol-Anon were broken. Efforts were made by Raxtie and most members of the three organizations to keep participation in the Santo Niño Devotion intact. Attendance to the Santo Niño First Friday devotions, participation in its activities, continued as it had been. Concerted efforts were exerted by most members to keep the Devotion uncompromised and untarnished by the interpersonal conflicts of a few individuals.

The Boholanos say today that there was never any intention to leave the Santo Niño Devotion. Through those trying times, it was quite evident that every First Friday and Fiesta, the Boholanos who had been active in the Devotion since the beginning, continued to be active and participating.

The reassuring and encouraging aspect, the moral of the story we might say, is that the majority of members in both organizations did not allow themselves to be dragged into the contentious terrain of the very few.

As we see now, the Santo Niño group has survived, its members and participants maturer and wiser. Hopefully. Raxtie and other Boholanos, who never broke their communication with important personages of the Santo Niño group during those trying times, focused their faith and confidence on those they saw as the truly devoted.

∾

Raxtie attributes his endurance through all those trying times from the lessons he learned when he went through the personal pain of deciding to leave the priestly ministry. One cannot go through a critically personal and spiritual decision like that and not learned the precious and rare ability to know oneself. Raxtie chose that critical period of his life to build, to fortify, what is naturally honest, caring and spiritually true about himself. The rich dramatic details of that time in his life is relevant only for his own personal narrative. Suffice it to say that whatever Raxtie had absorbed deep into his being from his priestly past, a past which he shares with other important personages in our Santo Niño story, has become one of the sturdy human and spiritual bricks laid on the foundation of the Santo Niño Devotion.

(Raxtie and Nenen have two children, Daphne and Arnie. Daphne designed the cover of this book).

∾

19

Images

Where and how we fell in love for the first time; where we found joy; where we were hurt; where we played as children. Our Philippine thoughts are filled with such images. But the image that never fades is where we learned to pray.

The pictures and statues of saints in the churches and in the altars of our homes are etched indelibly in our minds. These images replay in our heads like endless loops of film when we pray. These images beckon us to prayer, even during those times when we have forgotten how.

Prayers are emotional pleas, never invocations for intellectual discussions. We pray to praise, to ask favors, to express gratitude, to seek forgiveness, to atone, to appease, to unload burdens, even to question and be clarified. We pray during those times when prayers are the only words left to say, when it is the only consolation.

Worship is human passion leavened with ancient mysteries and folklore, driven by desires for salvation.

But passion can wax and wane. Recurring doubts and fading faith thin out our beliefs. That is when we reach the crossroads. Will we seek renewal, will we revive that special innocence which seeded our initial beliefs? Or, do we persist in doubts and indifference?

Through the years of the Santo Niño Devotion, we nurtured the hope that within the Devotion we can recapture that innocence to continue believing.

∾

For us Filipinos, the initiation of our catechismal pathways in Faith and Belief was ushered in with bold, multi-colored, tri-dimensional accompaniments. The life-like, life-sized images of Christ and the endless rows of Saints and Martyrs were burned into our consciousness. Each image was absorbed to be emulated, to be incorporated into our own developing self-image.

The embossed, graphic stages of the Way of the Cross.

A tall, stern-faced Jesus pointing to His Sacred Heart.

Our Lady of Fatima floating on pure white clouds.

Saint Sebastian pierced with arrows.

Saint Francis of Assissi gilded with perched birds on his arms and shoulders.

Saint Anne with the Child Mary on her lap.

Countless patron saints in all our hometowns, in mystical or martyred poses.

The haunting drama of the Passion of Christ.

The ennobling accounts of the lives of saints and the nightmarish fates of martyrs...

All these images embedded in our hearts and minds as we take our halting steps to our First Communion.

∽

Our human mind and emotion being what it is, we develop earthly associations with all these images. Memories of battery-powered toy cars, the pink sequined- dresses, the salty sweetness of Chinese ham, the apples, the grapes on Christmas morning, all cannot be separated in our mind's eye from the Nativity scene. It is too easy to picture the Child on the manger surrounded with toy trains and talking dolls.

In many Philippines towns, the annual Semana Santa, (Lenten Week), means banquets and the boisterous gaiety of family reunions. A whole congregation of family members, usually separated by time and place during the rest of the year, converge to take care of the family's traditional *caro* for the procession chronicling Christ's Passion. In this instance, the joyousness of families getting together is intertwined with the stark image of the life-sized, bleeding, tortured Christ in the Holy Thursday procession.

∽

With the recollection of those images comes the echo of the voices of grandmothers, mothers, catechism teachers, teaching us to pray. Those voices gave the words of the "Hail Mary", the

"Our Father," a personal human tone and timbre, a flesh and blood sound and meaning. Wherever we are, whenever we pray, those voices reverberate. During tragic and unfortunate times in our lives, the echoes of those voices can be the only redeeming, consoling sounds. At times, the only relief.

In English, in Cebuano, in Tagalog, in Bicolano, in Ilocano, in Spanish, in whatever language we learned to pray, in joy and in sorrow, we hold on to those voices.

We listened over and over and learned to recite those prayers in many places. In the cool corners of Spanish-era Philippine churches, the prayer words articulated in stumbling rhythms, accompanied by the chirpings of sparrows nesting on the church eaves. In the cozy living rooms of our homes, where we speeded up the prayer-recitation because playmates were beckoning outside. In chapels by the sea, with palm-leaf walls and roof, the prayers repeatedly recited with the sounds of endless dash of waves urging our struggles to remember the words like a demanding metronome.

When we pray, we intently, unblinkingly look at the colors, the textures, the faces of the icons we are praying to. Then we touch the bodily contours of the sacred statue, or the surface of the picture, as though on leaving, we carry with us a small part of the aura around the revered object. Seeing, touching the image we pray to, gives a sense that we have been heard, that we have made eye contact with the blessed and the divine.

Imagination is not enough. We are humans. We need to see, hear, touch, smell, taste. Even in prayer.

∾

20

Blooming Where He is Planted

It was a chilly Saturday in November 2003. Ed and Susan Bilbao were hosting an intimate wedding anniversary dinner for close friends and relatives at Heron Cove, a private Tampa clubhouse. By that time, the number of Filipino priests assigned to parishes within the Tampa-Orlando area was increasing. Most of them regularly attend and participate in the First Friday Santo Niño novena and mass.

As is usual at Ed and Susan's social gatherings, at least three or four Filipino priests are huddled in some corner of the room in lively conversation. That night was typical except for a new face among the familiar ecclesiastical and non-ecclesiastical guests. Amidst the laughter and the garrulous voices, this unfamiliar face stood out. Quietly he stood, just listening, with a smile that can be temptingly described as beatific. His eyes were slits of amusement. (Years later, that particular facial expression would become his familiar trademark).

That quiet, smiling person was, still is, Father Jose "Joy" Colina, unwrapped for the first time outside St. Paul Church. This was his social debut. Since that time, in the seven and a half years of Father Joy's tenure at St. Paul Parish, rarely was he absent in Filipino social and liturgical gatherings. The unifying effect of his personal warmth and pastoral counsel was quickly appreciated by the Santo Niño devotees and the Filipino community. His presence became increasingly sought after.

∾

For non-clerics, it is easy to forget that priests get lonely and have difficulties adjusting to new environments. We assume that the seminary has emotionally and psychologically shaped them to fit instantly in whatever place they find themselves. We have been narcissistically conditioned to look to priests for our own solace and comfort. We forget that priests also go through difficult times in their lives. We are heedless that they too can have moments when they need a sense of the familiar and the closeness of friends.

Just like any emigrant, Father Joy left the Philippines with all kinds of fantasies on what America would be. He thought America was just like what he saw in the movies -- bright lights, music, friendly people. What he found in his first few months instead was a lonely place. The vastly unfamiliar surroundings felt disconcerting, dislocating. The endless roar of traffic on Dale Mabry. The electronic chime from the belfry of St. Paul church, an every-thirty-minute melancholy reminder that he was not home. The eerie quiet of Stall Road late at night when he could not sleep. The undercurrent suspicion that as a non-White he was perceived differently. The longing to talk to some Filipinos which he suppressed because he did not want to bother the few whom he had met. Even today, seven and a half years later, the sights, sounds, smell of that time are still quite vivid. What he had absorbed in those early days will be in him the rest of his life.

He had met Ed and Susan and the other Filipino priests but they too had full daily activities. Always thoughtful and considerate, no matter how lonely he felt, he did not want to bother them. At the end of his pastoral day he would take walks along the edge of Dale Mabry until advised of the danger from rushing traffic. When somebody in the parish thoughtfully got him a membership at Bally Gym, fears for his life and limb eased. He continued a hobby he had in the Philippines, cultivating bonzai plants. When he saw that the live altar plant decorations were thrown away as trash even if they were still quite viable, he started picking out the ones he liked and replanted them in the parish garden. Like his bonzai, those would-have-been discarded plants are now thriving luxuriantly in the parish garden. They have become a living, greening testimonial that one Filipino priest, a horticulture hobbyist, once soothed his loneliness by recycling discarded plants.

It is easy to see those recycled plants at the St. Paul Parish garden as metaphors for us emigrants who have replanted ourselves, and, with great effort, send down roots in the new terrain as Father Joy has done.

∾

Father Joy came to Tampa on November 6, 2003 straight from the Philippines (with only a few days stay in California). He has never been outside the Philippines. The farthest he had been away from home was when he was in the seminary in Naga City, Albay (Holy Rosary Major Seminary, Nueva Caceres). He was ordained on March 11, 1989 at the age of 25. It is worth noting that the first informal celebration of the Santo Niño group at Ledy Colina's place in Plant City was on January 1989. Little did anyone know then that almost two months after that event, a person who would play an important role in the Santo Niño Devotion was being ordained in far away Albay, Philippines.

Father Joy's father died two months after he entered the seminary and his mother died a year before he left the Philippines. Being the oldest, even when he was already doing his pastoral work at St. Paul, he was still being consulted by his siblings regarding family matters.

His first assignment as a pastor was in Matakon, a barrio of the town of Polangui, just a few kilometers north of his hometown, Oas, Albay. In the six years that he was the pastor there, he visited his family often. In contrast to that was his initial few months in Florida, tucked away in that wooded corner of Stall Road and Dale Mabry. He could not be any more distant from home.

Immersing himself in his pastoral work facilitated his adjustment. There were aspects in that work however which needed a different approach from how it was done in the Philippines. Even the saving of souls, Father Joy realized, has to be fine tuned and recalibrated for cultural variations.

As time passed, Father Joy's contacts with the Filipino community increased. From his involvement with the Santo Niño group, he became the unofficial vicar of the Filipino community in the St. Paul parish vicinity and beyond. He became an integral part of the Santo Niño Devotion's various activities including being the main liaison with St. Paul Parish. That was a very important role when the serious planning for building the Santo Niño Shrine began.

To help all emigrants, not just Filipinos, ease themselves into their new home and culture became his personal and pastoral mission. He encourages everyone to keep most of the traditional way of worship practiced in the cultures left behind. He is convinced that this helps immensely the adjustment of emigrants to their new homes. Another important part of acculturization that Father Joy suggests is the carrying on of devotions people had in their home country, including physically bringing in the religious images venerated. Prominent illustrations of these, he points out, are the Santo Niño Devotion, the Bicolanos' devotion to Our Lady of Penafrancia and the Boholanos observance of the Feast of St. Joseph.

Father Joy went on to get deeply involved in the Filipino Ministry and in the Spanish Ministry, and, when needed, in the other cultural ministries. He is very appreciative that St. Paul parishioners are made up of people from many countries and diverse cultures.

The accomplishment that he is most proud of is his close work with the Santo Niño Shrine Building Committee. He has attended almost every meeting in the four years of the Shrine Building Committee's discussions, 2007-2010. In his close involvement with the Committee, he felt more confidence in his ability to restore peace when heated arguments threaten to disrupt the unity. He has always been particular about people being united and working together for a worthy purpose. He is also particularly happy about his work as the bridge between the Committee and St. Paul Parish.

The Committee's efforts and the help Father Joy has given in the completion of the Santo Niño Shrine have all been deservedly noted and stored in the Santo Niño Time Capsule including Father Joy's message, (in pure Bicolano), to the Santo Niño Devotees of 2061.

At last, for Father Jose "Joy" Colina, Tampa does not feel like "a foreign place," anymore. It is even acquiring the sight, sound, smell and taste of home. He believes this feeling to be the embodiment of his lifetime motto -- "One needs to bloom where he is planted." Like the many bonzai he cultivates, the altar plants he rescued, Father Joy has bloomed.

(On July 1, 2011 Father Joy started his new assignment at the Dunedin parish, a city along the shores of Tampa Bay, a hollering distance from St. Paul Church. At this writing, the new St. Paul Parochial Vicars are Father J. Glenn Diaz and Father Timothy Cummings).

21

Service in Perpetual Motion

It's 8:30 on the morning of the Fiesta. The January chill lingers like an over-staying visitor. Since she arrived forty-five minutes ago at the St. Paul campus, a petite Filipina has been criss-crossing the distance between the Church, the Family Center and the Pavilion so many times, she resembles the bouncing ball in a computer game. In these hurried, repeated, to-and-fro ambulations, she is never empty-handed. Now it is a big box twice her size, then a wide cardboard with pictures, in a few minutes a closed container with objects clattering inside. These gracefully borne over-sized objects she transports from building to building, in-between opening and locking up closets and store rooms.

This bundle of energy is Adela Gianan who knows where every box of plastic table covers, styrofoam cup, paper plate, plastic dinner ware, formal wine glasses and dinnerware are stored. If Adela does not show up on Fiesta mornings, there will be chaos looking for the Fiesta banquet paraphernalia.

It is not just her size which explains her ability to whiz from place to place. She seems to have an inborn mechanism to move fast, gracefully, good-naturedly. She moves and does her tasks always with a smile. Her friendliness and natural ability to connect with people has made her one of the truly dependable members of the Santo Niño Devotion. She is not only the person who knows where everything is stored, she also supervises the delivery of every object needed, most times delivering them herself. She also sings in the Fiesta Choir and dances in the Sinulog Dance presentations. In the 1997 Fiesta, there was an all-male Sinulog Dance presentation with her as the central, lone female dancer. They gave her a plaque for that.

∾

Adela is an Ilonga, born and raised in Miagao, Iloilo. The Santo Niño devotion is ingrained in her. For as long as she can remember, the church in her hometown celebrated the Santo Niño Fiesta every 3rd Sunday in January. The church in her hometown is one of the oldest churches in the Philippines. Going to that church with her family, year after year until she finished high school, is one of the vivid memories of her childhood.

Adela grew up with aunts. One of the aunts she lived with was married to a military man who ruled the family with rigid discipline. She remembers being resentful of him and his way of running the family. Assigned the responsibility of running a small store even when she was just in the 5th grade, she felt that she was being punished for offenses that she was not aware of. Later, as she started to experience the full impact of real life, she came to appreciate that discipline. She became aware that that was the kind of discipline needed to instill strength to bear life's demands. That early training has sustained her through all the stresses in her life.

After high school she went to Manila, living near Muntinglupa where she found a Santo Niño chapel with regular Friday devotions. She was very grateful for that because when she left her hometown she thought her Santo Niño devotion was ended. The focus of her prayers at that time was to find a life-improving job outside the Philippines. She prayed that the employment would not require some college credits because at that time she was only a high school graduate.

While waiting in Manila for any job opportunity outside the Philippines, she worked at a leather works factory. She was immediately assigned to work on a machine on which she was not trained. She decided to be honest with the supervisor and admitted she could not handle the job. Impressed with her honesty, they gave her a different assignment. From that position, from her willingness to learn new skills, she was promoted several times.

She knew her prayers were heard when in 1988, she had a job opportunity in Toronto, Canada.

In 1992, she had an opportunity to do the same work she had in Toronto in Tampa. She met Edwin Gianan and married him in 1995. Edwin is a brother of Nilda de la Cruz who, with her husband Tito were already active members of the Santo Niño Devotion. Within the first week of her marriage, she and Edwin attended the Santo Niño novena which was going on that week leading to the Fiesta. That started Adela's involvement with the Santo Niño Devotion, unbroken up to the present.

Since she joined the Devotion, she tries to be present on every First Friday novena and mass. Like any other regular, faithful devotee, she has memorized the words of the novena. If she is alone in her car, she places a small Santo Niño statue on the front passenger seat. She has this impression that when she is on her way to the Fiesta she never gets a red light.

Adela saw an extra blessing in her marriage to Edwin when she realized their close attachment to the Santo Niño Devotion. That feeling was strengthened when she quickly saw that she was welcome to participate in all the routine chores for all the activities, leading to the ever-moving Adela.

She also takes time to help Susan with soliciting contributions for the Devotion's Fiesta funds and encouraging parents to have their children join the Devotion. Her late husband Edwin, who was artistic, did a lot of art work for the various Santo Niño activities including printing the signs for the Fiestas. He even engraved "Santo Niño Shrine USA" on the silverware owned by the organization.

But the sun in Adela and Edwin's five-year marriage took on some dark clouds. It was racked with misunderstandings, ugly suspicions, unchecked impulses, all piling up, until solutions seemed beyond reach. They separated. When she learned that Edwin had been diagnosed with a terminal illness, she went to the hospital and stayed with him. They even went back together to their former home. For a little more than a month before Edwin died, they were a happily married couple again. "That brief time," Adela says, "was the best time of my marriage. We made the peace we failed to reach before."

Now we have the speedy, dependable Adela whom so many in the Devotion have come to rely on for all kinds of assignments. As if she is not busy enough in the Santo Niño Devotion group and in her regular job, she spends what free time she has doing pastoral care at St. Joseph's and Tampa General Hospitals. She also does Eucharistic Ministry at Christ the King Catholic Church.

But right now, on this bright Sunday morning of the Fiesta, she has one last box of dinnerware to take to the Pavilion.

Adela is one of the many who have become the trade mark personages of the Santo Niño Devotion, one of those faces that when missing, the group looks incomplete. She is also part of that choice group who has stayed with the Devotion steadily, faithfully, devotedly. In these times of unstable attachments, this kind of faithfulness deserves to be celebrated. In the current officer line-up, Adela is the PRO.

22

The Long Road to the Shrine

by Florenda C. Alquizola

Since the Santo Niño Devotion found its home at St. Paul Parish sometime in 1990, it has been customary for the officers and members of the organization to meet with the St. Paul Pastor in early December to present the liturgical and non-liturgical plans for the January Santo Niño Fiesta.

The meeting with Father Len Piotrowski, the Pastor of St. Paul Parish, in December 2006 at Ed and Susan Bilbao's residence was exactly that kind of routine. Father Jose Joy Colina, on his third year as Associate Pastor, was also present. By this time Father Joy had already become a close friend and attentive spiritual leader of the Santo Niño group.

The meeting that night in December 2006 was, as is usual in Filipino gatherings, preceded by the traditional Filipino potluck dinner. We Filipinos believe in being well-nourished before tackling meetings. As the meeting was winding down, Ledy Colina asked Father Len whether the Parish would consider the idea of the Santo Niño group building a Santo Niño Shrine inside St. Paul Church or on the grounds. Father Len sounded agreeable and encouraging. Hearing that kind of response from the Parish Pastor revived the long dormant dream of building a Santo Niño Shrine.

When the attendees of the Santo Niño Devotion progressively increased through the years, the desire to build a Santo Niño Shrine was always in the minds of the organization members. That is the reason why when the organization was incorporated in 1996, the official name became Santo Niño Shrine USA. But being people with a realistic, practical sense, such matters as expenses and logistics tempered the ambition and the dream. It was set aside as a distant dream, almost as many times as it was thought about.

Until that December night in 2006, when the Santo Niño members heard an encouraging word from a person of authority like Father Len. There was a someone, finally, who might truly help to make the dream possible.

∽

The following week, the same group of Santo Niño organization members met again at the Bilbaos. By this time everyone was eager to follow through the Shrine project. Financing being where everything begins, an ad hoc Building Fund Committee was formed to do the fund-raising. The members chosen were Ledy Colina, Jose Raffiñan, Ben Mosquera, Rene and Evelyn Bondoc, Ireneo and Helen Racoma, Tony Bayani, Cesar Cruz, Ed and Susan Bilbao and Florenda Alquizola. As the current president of the Santo Niño Shrine USA, Maria Raffiñan chaired the newly formed committee.

Jose Raffiñan suggested that everyone at the meeting donate $100 each to be deposited as seed money. This would be in an account separate from the regular Santo Niño USA account. The $2,000 initially raised as seed money was used to open the Santo Niño Building Fund account at Bank of America. I was appointed secretary-treasurer for the Building Fund Committee. Later, the families of Alan and Marilyn Navarro, Ed and Susan Bilbao made a pledge of $400,000 as their donation for the Shrine Project.

At the same meeting an architect was introduced by Jay Dompor and his parents, Gerry and Fatima. Jay, a graduate in architecture himself, was at that time doing his internship at the firm where this architect is a member.

In that meeting the members of the Committee inquired about the architect's professional fee to design the Shrine. The architect's answer -- "my services in making the design would be my personal gift to St. Paul Church but the cost of the architectural construction drawing will be billed accordingly to the Santo Niño Shrine USA." He further said that he could not mention an amount yet for the construction drawing because that would be computed as he does the work. The meeting ended with the committee members expressing their gratitude for making this architect's "design services" free.

⌖

The entire year 2007 and a large half of 2008 were not easy times. The meetings were long, tedious, and, at times, contentious. It could almost be the basis of an instructive manual on "How Not to Build a Shrine".

The Building Fund Committee was now meeting once a month, half of those were with the architect. Diverse ideas on the look and style of the Shrine were offered, discussed and presented to the architect. It was not until April 2008 when the architect came up with a "rendering sketch." The Committee Members agreed on that particular sketch. Father Piotrowski also approved.

But discordant voices were still expressed by members of the Filipino community who were not actively involved in the Shrine Committee. There were even those who tried to persuade the officers of the Santo Niño organization to divert the funds pledged for the Santo Niño Shrine Project to sites other than St. Paul including the Philippines. This caused more disagreeable discussions, which delayed important decisions from being made. There were even times when it was feared that these intruding factors would derail the project.

It was only through calm, cool-minded persistence from some members of the Committee and Maria Raffinan's patience, (and the guiding grace of the Santo Niño), that the Organization stayed focused on building the Shrine at St. Paul.

In the meantime, a vigorous fund-raising campaign was waged. Pledges were coming in from the officers and members of the Santo Niño organization, from devotees in the Tampa Bay area and other parts of Florida, and even from Filipino residents in other states. The goal was to raise $100,000 to add to the $400,000 pledged by the Navarro-Bilbao families.

⌖

The cost of building the Shrine was initially pegged by the architect at $600,000. The officers of the Organization thought this was rather steep considering that the proposed structure initially designed by this architect was only 500 sq. feet and the lot is owned by the Diocese, thus, does not have to be paid for.

This amount did not include the fees for the architect and the architectural construction drawings.

This $600,000 amount became another source of extensive, occasionally tense discussions. But the latest architectural renderings had already been accepted by the Building Committee and approved by Father Piotrowski. That being the case, the architect suggested in early September 2008 for the Bilbaos to meet with the financial officer of St. Paul Parish to deposit the Shrine building fund to the St. Paul Parish account.

At that meeting with the Bilbaos, the St. Paul finance officer objected both to the price of construction set by the architect and the architect's fees. The St. Paul financial officer considered both amounts too high.

The month of September 2008, all the way to the end of the year was a difficult time for the leadership and officers of the Santo Niño Organization. The professional relationship with the architect was unraveling. St. Paul's displeasure with the expressed expense for the Shrine had to be resolved.

It is a credit to Presiding Chairman Maria Raffinan's continuing patience and cool-headedness in navigating through the uncharted shoals of two difficult tasks the members of the Committee had to do – One, terminating the architect's professional services with the minimum financial damage to the Organization; Two, sustaining the Santo Niño Organization's special spiritual relationship with St. Paul Parish. Supporting Maria all the way were the unwavering enthusiasm and resolve of the entire organizational membership to go on with building the Shrine despite the delays and the distractions. The determined unity shown by this Committee is something rarely seen in an organization.

Having found its bearings again out of the rough seas, the Organization's next step was to hire a new architect. By the beginning of 2009, Mr. Alberto Portela came into the Shrine project.

From the beginning Mr. Portela was assisted by his wife Magda as the interior designer. Magda routinely does this for all their projects. Mr. Portela's conceptual view and thoroughness were quite evident when he first presented his initial ideas for the proposed Shrine. Equally reassuring was his thorough knowledge of the intricate steps that have to be gone through in obtaining approval from the Diocese of St. Petersburg to start any liturgical project. The Organization's first meetings with him and Magda put every one at ease. Confidence was restored that the Shrine would finally become a reality.

Up front, Alberto and Magda presented the Organization their professional fee of $29,000 and a construction estimate of $364,000 for the building of the Shrine. $325,000 would be for the actual construction and the rest of the amount for such details as the architectural elements, the structural, mechanical and electrical engineering services, interior design, landscaping, drainage permits, soil testing and peer review.

From March 2009 to December 2009 the Building Committee members met at an average of twice a month to sift through the intricate process of building a Shrine by committee.

Unlike the drawn-out aimlessness of the previous months, as soon as the Portelas settled down to the job, the members of the committee led by Maria Raffinan, quickly went into the minute details of what had to be done. The membership was stunned and thrilled to be exposed to so many details – from the Design and Development drawings to picking out the most appropriate colored tiles, ceiling Hardie panels, shatter-proof glass to enclose the Santo Niño statue, aluminum panels, air conditioning, contractor bids, landscaping, security cameras and granite benches. The Portelas saw to it that every member of the committee was fully appraised of every detail. The committee was even introduced to an entity mysteriously called DECLAA&E. This turned out to be not a musical term, nor a secret spy network, not even a vegan dish; this is no more exotic than the acronym for the Diocesan Committee for Liturgical Art, Architecture and Environment. Then, with the involvement of Mosaic Artist Anne Marie Kearney, the Committee's artistic learning process was further enhanced with the planning of the four mosaics to span the Shrine's wall.

With the formation of the Shrine solidifying, the Committee members went into more intense fund drives. Contributions from countless devotees of the Santo Niño trickled in to the building fund account. By the end of 2009 contributed checks had a total of $456,000, all deposited in the St. Paul Catholic Church building account. All these were to cover the architect's fees, mosaic art work and construction cost for building the Shrine.

∾

On a bright sunny Sunday, December 20, 2009, Ground Breaking took place after the 10:45 am Mass at St. Paul Church co-celebrated by Father Len Piotrowski, Pastor of St. Paul, and St. Paul Associate Pastor Father Joy Colina. For the first time, the Santo Niño statue which would be installed at the Shrine, was seen by the public. It was carried to the ground breaking site by Father Joy Colina and Tito de la Cruz, aided by other men devotees.

The Ground Breaking ceremony began with a brief introductory statement by Maria Raffinan, President of Santo Niño Shrine USA Inc. She then introduced the Shrine's Architect, Alberto Portela, Jr., who gave a brief statement. Father Len also gave a brief statement. This was followed with the formal presentation of the Santo Niño statue to St. Paul Parish by Ledy Colina who was doing it in the name of the statue donors, Demosthenes and Carmen Co who were snow-bound in New Jersey. The brief statements were followed with musical renditions by Joselito Reynes and Marilyn 'Neneng' Navarro, adding a moving, lyrical touch to the occasion. Marilyn's song in Cebuano titled "Santo Ninyo" (Cebuano for "Holy Child") is a musical prayer expressing praise and thanksgiving for the unceasing blessing bestowed on the Santo Niño Devotees. Joselito's song is titled "Find Us Faithful" (William Gurnall), a hymn about the inspiration pilgrims instill at all times, past, present and future. Both songs, heartily sung, were fitting musical expressions of the Santo Niño Devotion milestone established that day.

The actual ceremony began with the ribbon cutting by Father Len Piotrowski, Father Joy Colina and Maria Raffinan. Then picking up shovels and wearing yellow hard hats, the ceremonial Ground Breaking was performed by Father Len Piotrowski, Father Joy Colina and Father Joseph Musco. The symbolic shoveling of dirt and the burying of the equally symbolic time capsule by officers and members of the Santo Niño organization then followed. Quickly, a big crowd gathered inside the tent built over the shoveled site of the proposed Shrine. All were wearing yellow hard hats, all were shoveling dirt as they posed for pictures. As is usual, food and refreshment were served at the St. Paul Parish Pavilion after the ceremonies. (The actual Time Capsule containing comprehensive documents and pictures describing the Santo Niño Devotion's progression through the years was sealed with appropriate ceremony inside the Santo Niño statue pedestal on June 24, 2011 to be opened fifty years from that date).

Even if the contractual arrangement with the architect, the building contractor and the mosaic artist were all with St. Paul Parish and the Diocese of St. Petersburg, as it should be, the officers of the Santo Niño Shrine USA Organization were closely involved throughout every step of the design and building of the Shrine. They went through every detail of the contractual bids, the selection of materials for the roof, walls and floors. Philippine cultural and historical materials about the Santo Niño were gathered for the Mosaic Artist, Anne Marie Kearney.

From the start, the conception for the four mosaic panels was to depict artistically the themes of "Gather", "Nourish", "Sent", and "Led by a Child". These panels form a panorama on the wall of the Shrine, at the center of which is the statue of the Santo Niño. In captivating colors and design, the images on the mosaic tell the story of the Santo Niño de Cebu and a nation's and a people's pilgrimage.

Construction of the Shrine finally began in early 2010. By August 2010, the almost-finished building stood as the majestic concrete manifestation of a dream.

To celebrate the realization of this dream, on Friday, July 9, 2010, a dinner dance was held at Higgins Hall in Tampa, Florida. This was the eve of the dedication of the Shrine. (Realized dreams of this magnitude, being not inexpensive, this gala affair was also to raise funds). Some four hundred Santo Niño devotees and their guests, as usual dressed in their finest, dined, wined and danced. Celebrating with the Santo Niño devotees and organization officers were Architect Alberto Portela and his wife Magda, Father Len

Piotrowski, Father Joy, Father Musco and members of the clergy of St. Petersburg Diocese. Prominently present also was Monsignor Austin Mullen, the pastor of St. Paul in 1990 who first gave the Santo Niño devotees a home at St. Paul Parish.

After the nine-course Chinese dinner, the officers of the Santo Niño Shrine USA and the Santo Niño Building Fund Committee, led by Maria Raffiñan, were individually presented to the guests. The ladies in their resplendent gowns, and the gentlemen in their colorful, variously tailored variations of the barong, marched one by one as each was presented. Each self-conscious step, each unrehearsed smile shown on the way to the front, was felt as another lively reward for all those tedious meeting-nights putting together, piece by piece, the plans for the Shrine. As they lined up in front of the stage, glowing to the applause of the guests, they knew every minute of the meetings was well worth it.

Speeches by Maria Raffinan, the outgoing president of Santo Niño Shrine USA, Ed Bilbao, the in-coming president, Father Piotrowski, Architect Portela and Monsignor Mullen followed. The main entertainment of the evening was a choreographed dance, (by Joey Omila), re-enacting the presentation of the Santo Niño statue to Queen Juana of Cebu in 1521.

After the dining, the dancing, the jubilation, the gratified and gratifying speeches, $24,122 was raised for the Shrine's present and future expenses.

∿

The next day dawned bright and clear, as it has been in all these Santo Niño celebrations. By mid-afternoon, Saturday, July 10, 2010, Father Joy, Ed Bilbao, Tito de la Cruz were at Father Joy's parish office putting the finishing touches to the Santo Niño statue. Midst the excitement, the heavy metal crown of the statue fell on Ed's head, leaving a small laceration. Ed shed a few drops of blood for this momentous occasion, unintentionally carrying on a Filipino superstition that every important event should be marked with the shedding of animal blood to ward off misfortune.

The Santo Niño statue was then manually carried by Tito de la Cruz and Ed Bilbao, all across the distance from Father Joy's office to the Shrine, creating a private procession of three or four people. The glass enclosure at the Shrine was opened by Mr. Portela who checked the temperature control before Ed, Tito and Father Joy put in place the Santo Niño statue on its pedestal, on its sacred perch for the first time, and there to stay for all times. The majesty of the Santo Niño's physical, non-ceremonial placement was witnessed only by the few who physically helped, and by a few bystanders with cameras. Like most pre-ceremonial installations, this was marked privately, quietly, in the hearts of the few who were there, a moment they would always remember.

On that Saturday afternoon, July 10, devotees flocked to the campus of St. Paul Parish still flushed with Fiesta mood from the night before and the anticipation of the official dedication ceremony to come. Bishop Robert Lynch of the Diocese of St. Petersburg officiated at both the Eucharistic celebration and the dedication ceremonies.

Monsignor Lynch's homily elaborated on the theme of the Good Samaritan who stopped to help an injured man lying on a dangerous highway. He reminded everyone that at the time of this Biblical narrative, Samaritan was the label applied to an ostracized group of people, seen as "heretics and breakers of the ceremonial laws." They were hated by the religious establishment. As emigrants, Monsignor Lynch continued, the Santo Niño devotees could identify with being outsiders, a group ostracized by the establishment. Yet, like the Good Samaritan, emigrants through the years have worked to help those most in need. The Bishop cited some of the charitable work the Parish of St. Paul had extended to those most in need and the role of emigrants in making it possible. After the Mass, everyone followed Bishop Lynch to the Shrine for the Blessing and Dedication.

That night, after everyone left, the Shrine and the Santo Niño statue shone for the first time on the grounds of St. Paul, a beacon of peace and light in its very own corner. This Prayer Space is the result of the nurturing stewardship and generosity of Bishop Robert Lynch and Father Len Piotrowski and their predecessors. Their patience and inspiration were indispensable in sustaining the devotion of the Santo Niño within the St. Paul Parish family, giving the Santo Niño a home. The Devotion was strengthened more when, in November 2003, the Diocese brought in Father Jose Colina who provided additional tireless support.

Seven months after the Dedication Ceremony, the four mosaic panels by Artist Anne Marie Kearney were fully in view. Then the iron grill work and a matching metal fence around the building were put in place. This work by Metals and Nature depicts a natural motif of branches, leaves, birds and nests serving as candle holders rendered in metal.

∾

Most dictionaries of the English language have this entry on the word "shrine" – from the Latin "scrinium" meaning "a case or box for keeping papers." When taken to its religious connotation it means "a religious place built to remember a particular holy person or event; a place of respect because it is related to a person, an activity or event admired or held sacred." It is also "a niche, an enclosure containing a religious statue or other religious object."

Now stands a Santo Niño de Cebu Shrine in this corner of America, a symbol of the devotion of the Filipino community and its dream of sharing an integral part of their Catholic and cultural heritage with St. Paul Parish and the Diocese of St. Petersburg. Most Filipinos in the Tampa Bay area were brought up on this heritage. For scores of years, this devotional heritage had been carried on by thousands upon thousands of devotees who come to Cebu City every January to pay homage to the Santo Niño. Now this place of contemplation, this prayer space, this niche for everyone who seeks a moment of peace and hope, has come to Tampa Bay.

∾

23

The Sheltering Cape

"We make the world we inhabit," writes Novelist Ursula K. Le Guin. "We patch it together" from "the inexhaustible chaos of the real."

All of us have been on journeys and at our last stop we made new worlds to inhabit. Out of the "inexhaustible chaos" of our personal realities, we bestowed order and coherence on our new worlds.

One of these worlds we have made for ourselves is the Santo Niño Devotion and from that, building the Santo Niño Shrine.

The husband-and-wife creative team of Alberto and Magda Portela, the architect and interior designer of the Santo Niño Shrine, have been on journeys like ours. But their transport was much more perilous because they were children fleeing from the 1960 socio-political upheaval in Cuba. Uprootment is disturbing enough. Being uprooted as children, with the very real presence of violence, can change immeasurably a person's perspective on life. Alberto and Magda channeled that early life experience to a humanistic religiosity and artistic creativity, so smoothly blended that it is expressed as one voice.

When the Santo Niño group contracted Alberto Portela and Magda to design the Shrine, nobody in the group knew them personally. They also did not know a single person in the Santo Niño group. They were introduced by Jay Dompor, an architect himself, the son of Fatima and Gerry Dompor, long-time organizers of the Devotion.

The Santo Niño group saw Alberto as the personification of the professional contracted to design the Shrine, while Alberto saw the group members as clients whose projected structure was of a religious nature. That gave him more than an ordinary interest since his previous constructions were churches, other structures for religious activities and other non-religious projects. The religious structures include St. Mark's the Evangelist Catholic Church in New Tampa, the Parish Community Center of Christ the King Parish, renovation of St. Joseph Church at MacDill, to name a few. Also, as a member of the Association of Consultants for Liturgical Space and a graduate of the Institute of Liturgical Consultants, buildings for religious activities are his specialty.

(At this writing the Portelas had just finished the remodeling of the altar and sanctuary of St. Paul Church which was blessed and celebrated by Bishop Robert Lynch during mass on September 10, 2011. Both Alberto and Magda were present and introduced by Father Piotrowski before the liturgical ceremonies began).

Alberto and Magda had not worked with Filipinos before. They were vaguely familiar with the Holy Child of Prague but knew next to nothing about the Santo Niño de Cebu. They immediately went into in-depth research on the details of the Santo Niño Devotion in the Philippines in general, and in Cebu in particular. They searched the internet, talked to members of the Santo Niño Committee every chance they got and attended Filipino activities to listen and learn.

∾

The first thing Alberto does after he accepts a project is to know as much as he can the people who are going to use the finished building. "Who am I designing for?" is a question he always asks himself first. Way before he draws a single line, he wants to get an idea of the personalities, habits, likes and dislikes and the daily routines of the individuals who will live in the structure he is designing. He tries to imagine how they are going to use the building, what makes them comfortable, what makes them uncomfortable.

He tells a story of a client for whom he was building a private home. One of the many unusual things he had to do to get to know his project was to climb a tree because the client wanted a certain view from that level of the house.

Then he asks himself – "What is the meaning of what I'm designing?" In the case of the Santo Niño Shrine, he found his answer through getting to know the Filipinos especially the group's attachment to the spirit of the Devotion. His and Magda's immersion in this project soon turned into an intellectual and passionate involvement, not only with the project but also with the Santo Niño Devotion. Soon, the project felt personal, more than just another contracted job to do.

Through the course of the many meetings with the Santo Niño Committee, Alberto noted the group members' passion to have this Shrine built. Rarely has he seen this kind of collective personal passion about a project initiated by an organization. He saw that in the members' interactions, in the way they built and rebuilt their unity, in the way they sorted out their disagreements. As Alberto saw all these, he found himself absorbing it, as though all that desire to have the Shrine built was in the air everyone breathed. From that interpersonal fervor, an image of how he was going to design the Shrine began to take shape in his mind.

From the group's efforts to unite at the end of every contentious day, he saw a flock needing to have a place, a space to be together. The spread of the Santo Niño's cape became his initial inspiration on how to shape that space. He saw the cape as welcoming arms spread out as an endless invitation to get everyone to come in, to pray with one voice and be sheltered. The Santo Niño's spreading cape became Alberto's basic design matrix.

The curved design of the back of the Shrine he wanted to symbolize the roads that all of us have travelled on. Not only the Filipinos' journey but the journey of the Santo Niño Himself, initially from Spain in 1521, then all over the Philippines, and now all over the world where Filipinos dwell. He was also reminded of his and Magda's own journey. Like a musical re-statement of themes, this journey imagery is reinterpreted as story and history in the four panel mosaic designed and made by Mosaic Artist Anne Marie Kearney.

The image of welcoming arms led to the idea of the embedded footsteps at the Shrine's gate, a representation in stone of the footsteps of everyone who had ever taken the journey to seek the blessing of the Santo Niño since the Devotion began centuries ago. A sense of timelessness is evoked in the implied image of devotees endlessly going in, refugees seeking asylum of every kind, all the footprints leading to the Santo Niño.

Alberto has always conceived the building to be open, no enclosing walls. Walls imply seclusion and separation, backs turned to the world, a shelter for only a chosen few. That is not what the Santo Niño Devotion means. Alberto believes that buildings used in prayer and liturgy should teach and catechize. Its very presence and façade should continuously send out an evangelical message.

In the finished Santo Niño Shrine today, anyone who approaches can feel that openness, that feeling of being eternally welcome and embraced.

Alberto deeply believes that when he designs "the Lord guides my hand. I always feel something spiritual going on when I design," he says. He takes his time in conceiving his designs, letting the idea find its own way into its initial shape. In the case of the Santo Niño Shrine, what he saw in the devotees' convictions, what he learned about the cultural origins of the Devotion, became the germinating seeds for what was shaping in his mind.

It has been his experience that when he has focussed on an initial concept, at some unexpected time and place, in church, at the grocery store, in a restaurant, on a plane, a design takes shape in his head. Then he starts to put it on paper.

When the Santo Niño committee discussed the best way to inform people about the Santo Niño Devotion, two ideas were entertained – One, placing a book in the Shrine giving an account of the history of the Santo Niño Devotion in Cebu; two, a series of paintings at the Shrine depicting the Santo Niño history. All were considered impractical. Then Magda remembered working with Mosaic Artist Anne Marie Kearney at a project at Christ the King Church. When Anne Marie presented her idea of the four-paneled mosaic, everyone thought that was the best way to impart the meaning of the Santo Niño Devotion and the Journey Theme.

(Following Chapter is on Mosaic Artist Anne Marie Kearney and the Mosaic).

∾

There is a historical, religious and cultural affinity between Alberto and Magda Portela and the Filipinos which we must note.

In 1899, America got involved in a war with Spain in the Philippines after America won their war with Spain in Cuba the year before. American culture and politics were then introduced to Cuba and the Philippines at about the same time, placing the two countries under definitive American influence. Cuba and the Philippines were like two children brought into the American political and cultural household together. As both countries shed off their centuries-old Spanish breeding, they were learning the ways of America. In this latter re-orientation, Americanization made deeper roots in the Filipinos than in Cubans. For instance, speaking Spanish in the Philippines was quickly superseded with speaking American English. Cubans continued speaking Spanish to this day. This is how the Portelas and the Filipinos share that background in the history of their two countries.

Another affinity of sorts is in the time of coming to America. Alberto and Magda came to America in 1960 as children fleeing political chaos. Most of the Filipinos in the Santo Niño Committee came to America in the 1960s and early 1970s as professionals seeking further education. Just like the Cubans and the Filipinos at the beginning of the 20th century, Alberto and Magda and most Santo Niño devotees learned about American living about the same time in the 1960s. Such fortuitous affinities cannot be ignored, which probably explains why the relationship between the Portelas and the Filipinos in the Santo Niño group worked well. The integral element however lies in the way Alberto and Magda share with the Filipinos the same passion and emotional relationship with Catholic belief.

∾

Alberto and Magda met in a Youth Mass in Miami. It is that kind of mass with bongos, timbales and guitars. They got married in 1972. Alberto is a 1974 graduate of the University of Miami School of Architecture. Magda is a 1972 graduate of the Ringling Institute of Design in Sarasota.

About the many, many long hours, meeting with the Santo Niño Shrine Building Committee, Alberto now says "I met them as clients. Now we are friends. Magda and I value deeply that experience." Both have even developed a taste for some of the Filipino cuisine they had tasted during the countless pre-meeting dinners. Magda characterizes their work on the Santo Niño Shrine as "a project from the heart and of the heart." Alberto hopes his design of the Santo Niño Shrine will be the vessel to transmit the message of the Santo Niño Devotion.

24

Art as Spiritual Movement

Those of us who were not members of the Santo Niño Shrine Building Committee were not aware of Anne Marie Kearney. Not until the many public ceremonies for the Shrine began. But even in those occasions, when she was introduced, what was briefly seen was a tall, poised lady at the edge of the crowd, shyly waving.

The very first image of her for most people was at the ground breaking ceremony. Later, she could be spotted in the church during the novena leading to the 2010 Fiesta. During the Fiesta itself, she could be seen briefly weaving through the crowd. Unless a Santo Niño devotee has attended the Building Committee meetings, no Devotion member had heard her voice. Typical of the true artist, for a long time, for the majority of the Santo Niño group, she was an anonymous face in the crowd.

But now she is widely known as the artist who did the absorbing four mosaic panels at the Santo Niño Shrine.

In the beginning, as much as she could, she mixed quietly, unobtrusively, with the Filipino crowd during the novena and the prayers leading to the Fiesta. Through this she absorbed not only the Filipino culture but the spirituality of the Santo Niño group. What she experienced moved her. "I saw a deep devotion among the group members, a strong prayer connection," Anne Marie says. "Sensing a spiritual movement is very important in my art work. Being with the devotees during the novena, was quite an inspiration as I worked on the mosaics".

Whatever cultural and spiritual emanations she absorbed, she translated piece by painstaking piece into those colored stain glass and stones she used to create the four mosaic panels illustrating the journey of the Santo Niño Devotion. Those four mosaic panels have artfully, soulfully captured and tell the centuries-old Santo Niño story as nothing had ever done before. In glowing colors, the four mosaic panels tell the Santo Niño story plainly, in a language that goes straight to the heart.

Before she was involved with this project, Anne Marie knew only one Filipino family but was unfamiliar with both the Filipino culture in general and the Santo Niño Devotion in particular. The only Filipino she can remember was a friend who played the violin to accompany her ballet dancing at Christ the King School.

Anne Marie was recommended to the Shrine Building Committee by Alberto and Magda Portela with whom she had worked before on her first mosaic, the St. John Bosco and the Spirit of Community mosaics at Christ the King church in Tampa. When she got the Santo Niño assignment, she immediately put herself on a crush course on the beginnings of the Santo Niño Devotion in the Philippines and how the Filipino emigrants spread it all over the world. She talked to as many available members of the Devotion. She read everything she could find about the Santo Niño Devotion. Of course, attending the Building Committee meetings and the inevitable dining on Filipino cuisine, were enough tutorials on Filipino culture.

∽

A few years ago, at the Christ the King parish, her parish since childhood, she went into what she calls a "prayer based work." This simply means that whatever work one does, should always be imbued with prayers. Since then, when she starts any project, she asks the ones giving her the assignment to pray first, for the project, for everyone involved in the work and for those who will avail or use the finished product. She believes that when one prays, as one does a certain work, any work, the blessing that goes into the work will flow into whoever will avail of that work.

In her prayers she has what she calls her "meditation tree". The steps she was taught in meditation starts with closing oneself to outside perceptions, then concentrating on an image of walking, climbing a mountain, entering a cove where there's water, getting on a boat, arriving at a field where there is a tree where one finds and talks to Jesus, Mary and other Saints and Guardians. Not only does she try to follow these steps when she meditates but she finds herself putting that tree on her art work. For instance in the Santo Niño Shrine mosaic, on the first panel, (Gathered), is the image of Jesus under a tree talking to people. On the second panel, (Nourished), the tree image is in the palm trees depicting the Philippine Christianization. On the third panel, (Sent), the tree has two women interacting, consoling, praying together. The tree in her art implies a sheltering place, a safe place, a refuge.

For Anne Marie the imaging of her own private tree is where she meditates before she starts any work -- "spending a moment with my guardian" is what she calls it.

∞

When she was putting the mosaic pieces for the first three panels at the Shrine, the Santo Niño statue was not installed yet inside the glass enclosure. The day she started working on the fourth panel, the final one, she was so focused on what she needed to do that she went straight to her work area. Then she happened to look up and saw the Santo Niño statue already installed. She said to herself, "He is here now, with me, working. What an inspiration that was." That is indeed a mystical moment because the fourth panel has the thematic line of the Santo Niño story – "A Little Child Shall Lead Them."

There is a red pathway that flows through the four mosaic panels, a reflection of the Santo Niño red cape and a symbol of the paths that both the Santo Niño and the devotees have gone through. It is constructed to look like a continuous stream, a river of devotion, from one panel to the next. Between the second and the third panel is the Santo Niño statue, the very center of the Shrine. When Anne Marie was installing the second and the third panels, the statue was not installed yet. The second and third panels were bookending an empty space. She had no idea how tall is the statue, or what elevation it would have when placed on its pedestal.

When the Shrine was ready for the public, with everything in place, she went to see how everything looked. Then she saw something which really stunned her – the streaming red pathway going through the second and the third mosaic panels flows through the Santo Niño's red cape in amazing perfection, just as she initially conceived it. It gives an impression of the red colors streaming into the third panel, on its way to the fourth panel, as refreshed in its intensity from having gone through the statue's cape. This stunned Anne Marie because she never asked the people who were to instal the statue to put it at a certain height. She considers this as one of those coincidences for which no explanations should be asked, except to say "I'm a tool of what the spirit creates". She sees this as another manifestation of "the interweaving of faith and spirituality in artistic expression".

∽

During my conversation with Anne Marie, she was telling me very revealing insights on the interplay of art and faith. Then and there I realized that I could not do justice to most of what she was telling me unless she writes it in her own words. Happily, she consented to do that.

Another reason why I want to preserve her own words in this book is that we are really in a monumental time in our lives, in our Devotion. It is not often, in fact absolutely rare, that a small devotional group such as ours, succeeds in building a Shrine in their adopted land. And, like the rest of us, Anne Marie is as much a part of that very rare phenomenon.

In that Prayer Space we have erected, Anne Marie has placed an art work which will last for many, many life times. It is not just another commissioned art work. It is our story, the Santo Niño story, told in her original artistic vision. We must remember that just a few short months before she began her concept of the Santo Niño story, Anne Marie did not know us, she did not know Filipinos, nor was she familiar with the Philippines and the Santo Niño Devotion. But she made the mosaic which tells the story perfectly in all its emotional and devotional nuances. Prayer and Belief indeed are always with her in everything she does. And all that have been gifted to us in her art.

Here then is Anne Marie –

In Her Own Words.

"Working with the Filipino Community at Saint Paul's Catholic Church was a truly blessed experience. They were not only a wonderful, friendly people, quite inviting in the way they relate, but also a spiritually rich group. They blessed me with the opportunity to find the Santo Niño, an experience that has blessed, inspired and enriched my spiritual life and creative works".

"I began life as a ballet dancer and choreographer. I danced ballet from age 3 to 19. I studied with the San Francisco Ballet School when I was 13. When I was 14 I was an exchange student with an international ballet company and I was part of a summer ballet tour in Budapest, Hungary. I found myself in Sarasota, when I was 19, dancing with Eddy Toussaint. I then began to develop back problems and decided to follow my visual art path God was leading me to."

"I went to the Ringling School of Art and Design in Sarasota at age 19. I realized then that God continued to watch over me as I was led through wonderful experiences as a graphic designer, rug designer and fine art painter. I began to see God's path evolve. As a child, I would study the stained glass windows in church. To this day I find these stained glass patterns imitating through my work. In high school, and throughout my carrier, I found that I worked in little points of color. I studied pointillism in high school. I built rugs with pixels on the computer. All along the way, this was preparing me for the amazing world of creating mosaics."

"I graduated from the Ringling School with a Bachelor of Fine Arts, majoring in Illustration. Since then my experience ranges from Oil Painting, Acrylic, Ink, Watercolor, Pencil Drawing, Murals, Mosaics, Digital Fine Art, Graphic Design, Package Design and much more. My graphic designs use a fine art style and advanced color knowledge to create 'pop designs' for the competitive world of advertising and marketing. My digital artwork has ranged from designing Rugs and Tapestries to creating Fine Artwork for Private Collections. I specialize in creating large scale fine art stained glass mosaics. Other than the mosaics at the Santo Niño Shrine, some of my pointilistic illustrations can be viewed at Christ the King Catholic Church. I love using bright colors and strong, flowing compositions to tell the story of each piece of artwork."

"Creating God's artwork with beautiful tiny dots of vivid color filled with prayer, love and grace, is a blessing in my life. My work on Nature's Prayer, my first spiritual pointillism commissioned by Monsignor Michael Muhr, to the amazing Mosaics of the Santo

Nino Shrine at St. Paul's Catholic Church, have put me on my way to the Devotion through Grace Mosaic Series".

"I remember the first moment that my prayer and spiritual practices intertwined with my creative work. Monsignor Desmond Daly at Christ the King asked me to create a couple mosaics for the School and Community Center. Then the day came that I had to complete the face of St. John Bosco in small pieces of glass. I was taken back by the idea of building a face with pieces of glass. I knew that the only way to proceed was to get down on my knees and pray as I place every piece. It was then up to God to make the image appear. After a couple hours, absorbed in meditational prayer as I put together the image, I stepped back. And then and there I saw that St. John Bosco's face had taken shape, appearing in its entirety. I was overwhelmed. I was blessed with being part of a miracle. From that moment on I infuse every project with prayer. Every design is created, every material is cut and formed, and each piece is put in place within prayer. The idea has evolved since then and been enriched by the spiritual lessons I continue to learn and incorporate into my creative process".

"My spiritual teacher once taught me that when you cook food for your family, friends, the poor, and others in your community, you must always pray as you chop the vegetables and do all the preparations for the meal. The spirit of the prayers will be infused into the nourishing food and the people who eat the food will imbibe the nourishment of those prayers. I believe the same holds true for artwork. I believe God speaks through the Holy Spirit's creation of artistic works. Every piece of work I do is as amazing to me as it is to the viewer. I truly believe that I'm listening to the Holy Spirit when I create art and have God's blessings every step of the way."

"As I worked on the mosaic pieces for the Santo Niño Shrine, I detected a strong connection with a creative energy that felt spiritual, flowing freely. I believe that the power of all the prayers and novenas of the Santo Niño Devotees intensely flowed into the creation of the pieces. I have never felt nor heard such a powerful devotional pulse coming within the creation of a piece of art. The coming together of the mosaic pieces seems spiritually inspired, emanating a power full of grace."

"The Santo Niño has touched my life in a way I can never explain. I feel that He leads me through my personal life challenges and the amazing process of creating the Shrine mosaics with a kind and gentle, wise, confident hand. I have found the Christ Child to be an amazing gentle guide."

"Now let me tell you what's behind and what powers my work at JapaStudios which is a collection of artists creating spiritual art through meditation and prayer to inspire the viewer. Japa is a spiritual discipline involving the meditative repetition of a mantra or name of God. It is the soul of the artistic expressions created and shared through JapaStudios. The artists' works come from within their own explorations of their personal spiritual path and conversations with God. The pieces are then shared to inspire a connection between this spiritual interaction and the viewer of the art."

"I created the studios Mosaic Fine Artworks with James Michael Webb. Vivid color, unique design and spiritual inspiration are used to create the captivating fine art illustrations of JapaMosaics. These are one of a kind mosaics formed through artistic passion and meditative inspiration. Along with every prayer the pieces begin to unfold."

"It is said that the voice of God is often heard within an image. Through Artistic expression the Holy Spirit can be known and felt. Meditating with art strives to recognize these whispers from the Holy Spirit in an atmosphere of artistic beauty and quiet, fostering a deeper 'soul' conversation with God. We strive to find a capacity to move through and beyond to 'contact' God in a direct, personal way, creating a time of communion in which you can be inspired, healed, reconciled, challenged, and nourished."

"JapaStudios also supports many religious and spiritual humanitarian charities, inspired by Blessed Mother Teresa's words – 'I always begin my prayer in silence, for it is in the silence of the heart that God speaks. The fruit of silence is Prayer; the fruit of prayer is Faith; the fruit of Faith is Love; the fruit of love is Service; the fruit of Service is Peace.'"

25

Old Friends

Unlike the ones poignantly referred to in the Paul Simon song, these old friends are not yet ready to sit "on their parkbench like bookends." Through the years they have sat instead through many meetings, novena cycles and fellowship meals for the Santo Niño Devotion. Their closeness to each other is brought about by many shared life experiences, the lessons from which they have channeled into their services for the Santo Niño Devotion.

The pattern of this friendship spreads out, like roots of varied plants connecting, to form a network of mutual support. My wife Florenda's and my friendship with Ledy and Ernesto Colina began in Huntington, West Virginia in 1967. That friendship expanded with Beeboy and Helen Racoma in 1973. Beeboy and Ledy already knew each other being from the same town, Carcar, Cebu. Rolly Barcenilla, also from Carcar, is Beeboy's childhood friend. Rolly's wife Connie and I are from the same town, Barili, Cebu. Ledy and the Bondocs, Rene and Cherry, have been friends since their medical school days in Cebu City. Beeboy and Helen became friends with Bert and Lita Ortiz here in Tampa. When all of us moved to Tampa, with the Barcenillas in Orlando, this group coalesced around each other and around the Santo Niño Devotion.

This group has participated in Santo Niño activities in many ways – from grilling meat and frying lumpia during the days when St. Paul Church still held a fund-raising carnival; serving meals at the Fiesta banquets and serving ideas and suggestions in the various committees; leg work, phone work to raise funds. It was not uncommon in the past to see Ledy helping to set up glass and dinnerware for the priests' special table during Fiestas. Or Helen, a numbers whiz, sitting down with Susan and Nilda, to crunch numbers. Or Ledy, Flor, Helen, Lita and Cherry, with husbands in tow to do the heavy-lifting, coming in on cold January mornings to set up tables for the banquet at the pavilion. Or, lately, Flor and Helen helping Ed and Susan monitor the upkeep of the yard and railing around the Santo Niño Shrine. And who can forget Cherry enthusiastically selling commemorative calendars at the 2011 Fiesta. Then, at the end of the day, with everybody else, they go to yet another meeting.

An organization like the Santo Niño group is rarely a product of one glorious, masterstroke from one individual. Its core structure is put together with the small and large endeavors patiently put together by individuals. These "old friends" are among those individuals. At this point in time, as "Old Friend" Rene Bondoc says "Not only have we become a Family, we have also become unofficial missionaries because every time we celebrate, every time we do the First Friday novena and mass, we are spreading the Santo Niño Devotion."

This kind of faithful service to the Santo Niño Devotion, born from "old friendships", is repeated many times over among the other members of the Santo Niño group. They are the shifting, moving parts, making up the quiet engine inside the Santo Niño organization. Therein lies the simplest explanation why this organization has become a Family -- It is put together and sustained by groups of friends, "old friends", whose closeness with each other is felt as flesh and blood relation. As Irish poet W. B. Yeats says – "Think where man's glory most begins and ends, And say my glory was I had such friends".

26

A Brief Musical Interlude

In the mid-1990s, the Santo Niño Devotion was attracting more participants giving rise to more activities and more decorous celebrations. With its occasional temporal and liturgical excursions into glamour and grandeur, there came the need for music and dance. This brought into prominence some group members with special talents.

One of them was TQ Solis who came to Tampa in 1992 from Chicago. Being from Loay, Bohol, he already had a close relationship with the Boholanos in Tampa such as Raxtie Auza. TQ, is a musician and composer whose considerable skill is much more than the usual weekend piano tinkler. He was a multiple prize-winner in Cebu Metropop, a highly reputable competition for original compositions open to competitors from the Visayas and Mindanao. He won the top prize in 1983 with Damgo Man Lang, (Only A Dream), a lyrical ballad which has become an instant classic in the Philippines, frequently performed live, and recorded by individuals, orchestras and choral groups. In 1982 he took Second Place in a competition for original carols competition.

The fifth of seven siblings, every one in his family is a musician. A sister in Bohol is one of the organizers and the piano accompanist for the Loboc Children's Choir, a multiple prize winner in the Philippine National Music Competition for Young Artists and also in international competitions such as in Spain in the early 2000. A brother plays jazz in a prominent club in New York where big-name jazz artists hang out after hours.

A true original, TQ's talent is instinctive. He composes from the simple need to do so, the periodic compulsion as urgent as the need to breathe. Close friends are used to him getting up from the group in the middle of an exciting conversation, going quietly to a corner by himself, then coming back with a new song on a napkin or some scratch paper. Then, when tried later on the piano, those scribbled notes on a scratch paper is another lovely, entrancing tune.

Raxtie Auza got him to join Ang Bisaya and when his special talent was revealed, he was asked to organize a choir. Confident of his ability to shape a presentable choir from amateur voices, when potential members asked what qualifications he was looking for he said in Bisayan – "Basta dunay baba ug dunay tingog nga moguwa" (Anyone with a mouth that has a voice). And indeed, from a very diverse assortment of voices and spectrum of abilities to carry a tune, TQ organized an impressive choir which performed in one Fiesta High Mass, one Ang Bisaya gala and some private social occasions.

The reality of people's lives and expectations however got in the way of the choral group ever becoming successful. The choir slowly disintegrated. First and foremost, it was difficult to get members together for rehearsals because all were working or raising families with small children. TQ, already working in Ocala at that time, was himself also a major factor. It was getting difficult for him to be driving back and forth.

Among the Santo Niño members, it is common knowledge that some individuals who have consistently exerted efforts to keep the group together were once in the priestly ministry. We can even safely say that it is because of that very special part of their lives that their dedication to the Santo Niño Devotion has been well sustained.

TQ, who once taught a few of us to raise our praying voices in song, is now a nurse, a husband and a father of a daughter and a son. Even if TQ's stay with the group was such a brief musical interlude, he has kept his personal nearness to the Santo Niño Devotion, never failing to attend the Fiestas. He continues to use his talents to express spiritual yearnings and gratifications in music. He still composes reflexively. Currently a number of his compositions are being put together for a CD album. They are love songs but in-between are those special category of love songs – unadorned, deeply-felt prayers.

This is the kind of musical talent which once, all-too-briefly, provided melodic reverberations around the many Santo Niño celebrations. TQ's once selflessly contributed musical interlude, the echoes of which are now inaudible, is a small rock-marker among the many milestones along the road in this Santo Niño journey. It merits a knowing and wistful glance.

27

Dancing to Grace

"When there's something the Lord gives you, enjoy it," is Jose 'Joey' Omila's personal slogan. Most of his life, one special something the Lord gave him, which he enjoys expressing is dance. Dance, for Joey, expresses emotions, ideas, life's views, spiritual beliefs and prayer more fully than words. The embodiment of this belief Joey gave to the Santo Niño Devotion when, in its early years, he started the Offertory Dance during the Fiesta High Mass. Since then this has become an integral part of the liturgical observance of the Fiesta.

Joey is one of the earliest members of the Santo Niño organization. In 1986 he was a member of St. Paul Parish, active in the parish Men's Group. There he met Ed Bilbao who invited Joey to join the Santo Niño group when it was organizing in 1990. A sociable, charmingly engaging person, Joey quickly became an active participant in the increasing Santo Niño Devotion activities.

After having held a few Fiestas at St. Paul, Joey saw the celebrations becoming more elaborate. As a former member of the Philippine Bayanihan Dance Troupe, and, always conscious of propagating Philippine artistic culture, he suggested putting together a cultural dance which he volunteered to choreograph. He conceived it as a colorfully costumed, elegant dance-narrative, performed by about fifteen dancers. The choreography would illustrate in dance the bestowing of the original Santo Niño statue to the Cebu royalty by Ferdinand Magellan in 1521. The first time it was presented in a Fiesta High Mass was in the Fiesta of 1993. It was a big hit. Since then it is known as the Offertory Dance, performed at every Fiesta Mass.

Here is a brief description of Joey's creation. There is that few minutes of reflective silence which follows the celebrant's homily and the recitation of the Prayer of the Faithful. Then the prayerful hush erupts with the rhythmic booming beat of a wooden drum, the robust groan of a beaten hollowed tree trunk. The church middle aisle fills up with beautiful young people in lushly colored 16th century Philippine costumes, gracefully swaying and soft-stepping on their bare feet to the altar. In their midst is a young woman sitting on a woven bamboo palette on the shoulders of husky men in silky loose pants and sleeveless vests with pre-Hispanic designs. The young woman is carrying a small statue of the Santo Niño. (Some years the young woman role changes into a pre-teen boy).

The choreography is from Joey's imagination but the costumes and the drum beat he had thoroughly researched from descriptions of pre-Hispanic ceremonies in the island which is now Cebu. For years of Fiesta celebrations, through this historical artistic interlude in the middle of the Mass, Joey has infused a theatrical sense into the Santo Niño Devotion.

A few years back, a group of lively, graceful septuagenarians formed themselves into a Sinulog dance group. They called themselves the Golden Girls Dancers. Joey choreographed their stylized Sinulog moves, calibrated to take into account their very senior joints. They performed on several Fiesta afternoons. There was also that time when Joey was asked to give the regular Sinulog dancing at the Family Center some artistic touch, even turning it for a brief while into a dance group competition. Generally frowned upon because it was seen as taking away the spontaneity of prayer, (the true nature of the Sinulog dance), the competition part was short lived. There are still organized, rehearsed Sinulog dances performed but without the competition, staged purely for mutual entertainment.

After graduating with a degree of Fine Arts from the University of Santo Tomas in Manila, (awarded Most Outstanding Student of the Year 1970), Joey immediately went into the Philippine world of dance culture and art -- he joined the Philippine Bayanihan Dance Troupe in 1970. That Dance Troupe acquired international fame when sometime in the 1950s they performed to world acclaim in Broadway, even staying for a long run. Since that Broadway success, year after year, the Troupe travelled all over the world. Joey became a part of that from 1970 to 1977. After that he travelled all over Europe for Philippine tourism, studying German, (which he still speaks fluently), in his spare time. He smoothly went into studying German because his mother is a full blooded German but born and raised in the Philippines. It was through this linguistic expertise that he met Baron Arndt Krupp, a scion of the famed German steel family, the Krupps (see William Manchester's book, "Arms of Krupp", 1968). Joey was asked to interpret for the Baron when he was visiting Manila. He impressed the Baron so much that he appointed Joey as his family's Lord Chamberlain at their many palaces in Strasburg, Austria. Joey held this job for eleven years until the Baron's death in 1986 at the age of 49. Of the many services he did for the Baron and his family in those years, Joey is proudest of the fact that he was largely instrumental in the Baron's conversion to Catholicism, a ceremony done in Manila by the late Cardinal Sin.

Joey's exposure to the life of European royalty has not tarnished his consciousness of Philippine culture. Instead, because of the ways art is used in Europe to entertain and educate the general population, his interpretation of the dance in Philippine culture has become more elaborate and refined.

As he settled in Tampa after the Baron's death, Joey gradually became an important initiator and motivator of Tampa's Philippine cultural scene. He organized the Philippine Performing Arts Company, an interpretive dance troupe of Philippine native dances (he is still the Executive Director and choreographer); he was the Founding Director and Director of Cultural Affairs for the Philippine Cultural Foundation, Inc. for many years. (Now he is the Cultural Adviser).

Joey has many functions in many Tampa and St. Petersburg locations. When he is not being the choreographer of those artistically translated Filipino native dances, we see this man from Paray, Cotabato as a consistently articulate, refined and witty Master of Ceremonies in many important Filipino celebrations. Also, he used to be that friendly and accommodating travel agent, the man who could get us on a plane for the Philippines in a matter of hours when we have emergencies. As the face of the Philippine

Cultural or Bayanihan Center in its early years, he used to remind us of the many Filipino cultural events at the Center. But we know Joey most of all as a steady devotee and worker for the Santo Niño Devotion.

The awareness that Philippine culture is inextricably woven into the way we worship is deeply ingrained in us. Since the beginning of the Santo Niño organization, Joey has consistently strived that in the way we pray, there is always the semblance of a Philippine cultural atmosphere.

28

Stories, Visions and Answered Prayers

Engrossed in the rhythm of the Santo Niño novena on a First Friday at St. Paul Church, you happen to glance around and glimpse the praying faces. Unwilled and unbeckoned, images start to play in your mind's eye.

The faces of your fellow-devotees turn into the faces of people who mean something in all the seasons of your life -- your parents, your brothers and sisters, your schoolmates, your co-workers, your friends and lovers. Then, like a slide show that clicks on to the next frame, the faces turn back to that of your fellow devotees. In this Devotion, split-second visions like these are occasional reminders that our common past and our common present are shaded and tinted with similar colors. Despite our petty prejudices, our views, ideas and tastes have more in common than differences. The transgressions we commit are identical. So is the redemption we seek.

Through all the years of our being together, we have seen that the vitality of the Santo Niño Devotion comes from those who spend their days taking care of the sick, the young and the aged; from those who clean houses, shopping malls, wait on tables or serve drinks; from those who answer phones and have their fingers glued to computer keyboards, from those who oversee the workings of hospitals and businesses, direct vehicular traffic, teach school, raise families, construct houses, move and lift heavy objects.

The Santo Niño devotee is anyone and everyone.

In thinking about the rich diversity of the Santo Niño devotees, we must remember that some individuals who have been consistently devoted to their responsibilities to the Santo Niño group were once in the priestly ministry.

These individuals gave a lot of themselves to forge the strength that has built the Devotion. That unique spiritual gift they received in their past lives has evoked in many a steady dedication to the Santo Niño Devotion. Their contributions to the Devotion are incalculable. Not only have they organized the group, they have strived to keep it together when the group was beset with human folly. They have shared their special talents to give us the grace and comfort of music. They have given colors to our celebrations. Our appreciation of their efforts has awakened and enhanced our appreciation of each other.

But what must not be forgotten is that leaving the priestly ministry was not as easy as getting off a bus. Those of us who have never felt any ecclesiastical and pastoral calling can never imagine the personal and spiritual torment these fellow devotees went through when they were deciding to leave the Melchizedekian confines. Needless to say, the spiritual gifts these individuals have given us as individuals, as a community are immeasurable. To appreciate fully their contributions to our Devotion can only be done by tapping into our more enlightened nature, if only to have a shadow of an insight about that all-too-human decision they had made.

One thing these individuals have instilled in us is to continue listening to each other. Our stories are as endless as the unfolding of our daily realities. Occasionally, in the midst of our daily ordinariness, we find uplift and inspiration, we see visions, we look for apparitions, we see small favors and narrow escapes as answered prayers, as small miracles. And we must never cease to tell each other about it because in the telling they become real, in the sharing the Divine feels humanly reachable.

Here are a few of the stories.

∾

Known as a Eucharistic Minister for one of the Sunday masses at St. Paul and on the Santo Niño First Friday masses, Lisa Kenyon has a wide group of friends and acquaintances in the Santo Niño Devotion. Being a Eucharistic Minister was something she has always wanted to do since her arrival in Tampa in 1992. The opportunity came when Nan Garabelis, a regular Eucharistic Minister at St. Paul, moved with her husband to New Jersey sometime in the mid-1990s. Already active in the Filipino ministry at St. Paul and in the Santo Niño Devotion, Lisa was readily accepted to replace Nan.

Lisa's life is a series of answered prayers which she tells in exciting details. Born and raised in Butuan City in Agusan, Mindanao (Southern Philippines), she graduated from a midwifery school in Pangasinan. After graduation, while working as a private midwife, she heard of a nanny job in Saudi Arabia. What followed were a series of thrilling, on-the-edge developments involving applications, long lines of applicants, passports, birth certificates, bureaucratic slip-ups and other labyrinthine Philippine procedures created to make everything difficult.

In a series of frustrating, seemingly desperate, red-tape entangled moments, Lisa resorted to prayers. She would stop at every church on her way to all the requisite Manila bureaucratic offices. At the end of the day, scraping what little loose change she had left for bus fare, she unfailingly went to the Church of the Black Nazarene in Quiapo. (A district in Manila). There were times when she had no money left for bus fare and had to look for discarded bus tickets which had not been punched fully and could still passed for new.

Her prayers were answered and she got the Saudi nanny job. She took care of two Saudi boys, ages 3 and 2. Lisa made friends with the 11 other Filipinos working in that compound in Jidah. The family she was working for was so impressed with her work and her personality that they kept asking her to become a Muslim. They even took her to a pilgrimage in Mecca, dressed like any female Muslim pilgrim. She prayed with the family. But every time they asked her to become a Muslim, she would always say – "I can never turn Muslim. It is a religion without the Virgin Mary. If you force me, it would be useless because the moment I leave this country, I will not be Muslim anymore." The head of the family then said, "Lisa, you're the most honest, strongest but stupid person." She had a three-year contract but stayed for seven years, five of those working in a clinic as a midwife.

She went back to the Philippines in 1987 with the intention of becoming a nun. She actually inquired what she had to do at the Hospicio de San Jose Convent in Manila. But her father was adamant in her not becoming a nun, stubbornly refusing to sign the parental consent. In her frustration, she went to Hongkong, again to work as a nanny. She found out that the Chinese mothers were very difficult to work for. With Filipino friends, she frequented the Catholic churches because that was where they found peace, companionship and consolation with each other.

Encouraged by what the other Filipinas were doing she went into penpalling. This led to getting to know Lee Kenyon. The first time she saw Lee's picture, she wondered in her prayers what her fate might be with this man. Then an event that seems to be from the movies happened.

After she and Lee had been exchanging letters for five months, shortly before her birthday that December, she prayed that if on her birthday she receives roses from Lee and it snows in Hongkong, then Lee is her fated partner. Lo and behold, at 5 pm that day, she received roses from Lee and at 7 pm it snowed in Hongkong.

In February 1991, Lee visited her in Hongkong, stayed for four days, then proposed. They were married in Manila in August 1992. After Lisa came to Tampa in 1992 to join Lee, there were other trials. When she was three months pregnant, she was in a car accident. She and the child were not hurt. Everything that has gone well in herself and her family, she attributes as answers to her prayers.

Lisa continues to be actively involved in the Santo Niño Devotion. Her son, if not serving mass as one of the regular altar servers, is usually at the basketball court with Scotty Navarro.

∞

Thelma Mix, a long-time Santo Niño Devotee, has seen many aspects of her personal life, her survival through many adversities as blessings from the Santo Niño.

Thelma is from Bonifacio, Misamis Occidental (Southern Philippines). Not being from Cebu, she was unfamiliar about the Santo Niño Devotion. When she was living and working in Manila, her regular devotion was the Wednesday Perpetual Succour novena at Baclaran and frequent visits to the Black Nazarene church in Quiapo, a widely followed devotion in Manila.

Her introduction to America was at Chicago O'Hare International airport in 1990 when the friend who was supposed to meet her failed to do so. This began Thelma's fated encounters with the kindness of strangers. She did not know how to use the phone to call her friend. She only had $150. A man, a stranger who noticed how lost she was, allowed her to use the phone in his office to call her friend, then arranged for her to be transported to that friend's place for only $50. A cab would have cost her at least $80. Not long after, she found a job in Chicago.

Her next America was Las Vegas where she worked as a poker dealer. She had a relationship with a man who had a successful car repair shop but had a serious drug problem. After exploring all means for this man to get off drugs, Thelma thought, as a last resort, to get out of Vegas. The man consented to come to Tampa because his parents lived in St. Petersburg.

They moved to Tampa in 1993 with Thelma pregnant with her youngest child, the now 17-year old daughter. The man's drug use worsened. Thelma did not know a single soul in Tampa. She met Jerlyn, a Santo Niño devotee who introduced Thelma to the Bilbaos. Through these new friends Thelma was taken to a prenatal clinic.

A vivacious person who easily makes friends, through the Bilbaos and Jerlyn, her circle of friends widened, especially with those who were active in the Santo Niño Devotion. At that time Thelma knew that her new friends were blessings given at the perfect time, especially when the man she moved to Tampa with left, taking her money and everything she had. So there she was, new in Tampa, pregnant and with two boys to raise, abandoned in an unfamiliar place. Thelma attributes her survival on the unconditional help from her new friends and getting into the Santo Niño Devotion.

Her personal life slowly stabilizing, Thelma became closely and deeply involved with the Devotion, accepting whatever assignment needed to be done. She runs errands to pick up assorted items for the Fiestas. She sings in the First Friday novena and Fiesta choir. She choreographs the dances and organizes the dancers for the Fiesta Sinulog.

In the days leading to the 2004 Fiesta, she thought she would not be able to do the Sinulog dance. In 2000 she was in a bad car wreck which left her with severe chronic back pains. It got to a point where she had difficulty walking and sometimes could not stand up from a squatting or sitting position. During the 2004 novena nights, her back and lower extremity pains continued. She kept praying for relief so she could attend to her Sinulog dance assignment. After one novena night, as she was getting ready to walk to the Family Center from the church, she felt a sudden warmth on her left leg spreading up all the way to her hips. When she reached the Family Center for the dance practice, about a minute and a half walk from the church, she was fully free of pain. That night, she led the rehearsals of the Sinulog Dancers all the way to the actual Fiesta Sinulog.

These days, as she had been in the many years of Santo Niño celebrations, Thelma is one of the many energetic, enthusiastic, joyful members seen moving endlessly around, assisting to get all the big and small chores for the group done on time. Thelma, having brought about stable lives for her two sons and daughter as a single parent, has herself found a Home in Tampa and a Family in the Santo Niño Devotion.

She is now in the Board of Directors of the Santo Niño Shrine, USA, Inc.

∿

Laura Kuechenberg, a consistent participant of the Santo Niño Devotion from its early years, is from Palompon, Leyte. Even if always ready to give a helping hand, she prefers to remain in the background. She, Thelma and Imelda are rarely far from Susan's side especially when multiple tasks are to be done within a very limited time. These three ladies, in their quiet, unobtrusive way of doing things, have facilitated many schedules to be finished on time.

Laura's schooling was in Manila where she finished her accounting degree. She finished her MBA in the U.S. From 1980 to 1988 she was teaching in Thailand, enhancing her cultural orientation. That was where she met her husband.

She has a number of positive developments in her health which she attributes to her devotion to the Santo Niño. She sees all of them as answered prayers.

In 2000 she had severe ear pains which ear specialists attributed to a "hole in her ear drum." The only solution, she was told, was for the deficiency to be surgically patched, a procedure which she dreaded. Like most problems in her life, she prayed for some spiritual intervention. The next time she saw the specialist, no defect in her drum was seen. No need for any surgery.

A few years later, shortly before a Fiesta celebration, she was found to have lumps in her breast. Naturally, proper medical-surgical interventions were recommended, which again she dreaded. During the Fiesta, she quietly asked Father Jude Vera to pray with her as they did the Sinulog. When she went back to the doctor after the Fiesta, the lumps were gone. Laura considers all these turn of events as personal miracles granted to her.

Having been around the Devotion for many years, Laura has seen from the sidelines the interpersonal problems which occasionally threatened the Santo Niño organization. She really believes that prayer is the reason why those problems were resolved and the Devotion lived on. Whenever she hears derogatory comments on how the organization is managed, or about specific personages, instead of responding and arguing, she prays silently for those individuals to arrive at a clearer view. She always maintains enough faith that sooner or later, people will acquire a more enlightened view. Laura says she always tries to keep a positive view of her life and about everyone, a view she imparts to her two teenaged sons and twenty-two-year old daughter.

Mercie Bilbao is from Matag-ob, Leyte who lives and works in Vancouver, British Columbia. She left the Philippines in 1999. She is close to the Santo Niño Devotion and frequently visits Tampa because her son, an only child, goes to school here, living with her brother, Ed Bilbao, during the school months. When she had her divorce, her son was two and a half years old. Her main worry at that time was her son growing up without a father. This concern turned into serious worry when one day, picking up her son in school, she saw him hugging closely a classmate's father.

In 2002 she visited her brother Ed in Tampa whom she had not seen for twenty years. It was a joyful, touching reunion. She saw that her son quickly engaged with Uncle Ed and Auntie Susan. He also got along well quickly with an older cousin. She was so moved when Ed and Susan offered for her son to stay during the school months. She has always prayed that the trauma of her divorce will not leave too much of a disruptive effect on her son.

Her son's joyful attachment to his uncle and aunt, including being an active altar server for the Santo Niño Devotions, is an answered prayer that has given peace and solace to Mercie. Every chance she gets, she visits him here in Tampa. When school is out, he is with his mother in Vancouver.

That young man is familiar to the Santo Niño Devotees. Not only is he a regular altar server, he is one of the young people granted the privilege of preserving their footsteps in concrete and colored beads, together with Bishop Lynch's and Father Piotrowski's, at the gate of the Santo Niño Shrine. That young man with his intelligent, wittily animated facial expression, we know as Jasper. Mercie's prayers for her son to grow up in a family is twice answered – Jasper is also growing up with the Santo Niño Family.

When Tranquilina was growing up in Cebu City, she felt that only the rich people mattered. They were everywhere she looked -- in stores, offices, driven around in their cars to school, sitting in their special pews in church. Their lives were written about in newspapers, their pictures frequently publicized. Their statements were quoted with awe and respect. She felt that the poor, like her family, were faceless.

It was bad enough that there were days when they did not have much to eat in the house. There were also the violent fights between her parents, always ending with her mother beaten up by her drunken father. Her father had a habit of drinking away most of his earnings.

Many were the times when after a severe beating her mother would flee to a neighbor's house for the night. But in the morning she was unfailingly there to get Tranquilina and her brothers ready for school, and, on Sunday mornings, to get them ready for church. It was always like that, no matter how violent was their fight Saturday night -- her mother was there in the morning, with clean well-ironed clothes for her and her brothers so they could be at Mass on time. Some Sundays, only the children went to Mass because her mother's face and arms were swollen and badly bruised.

There were times in church when Tranquilina found herself murmuring -- "What have we done that we're starting life in this kind of home?" Then she would feel bad, afraid that God might think she was blaming Him.

The situation never got better. Her mother got sicker and within a few years she and her two brothers died. She was left with her father. The drinking was worse. Tranquilina was now the object of his beatings.

To get out of the situation, at age of 18, she married a young man she knew since grade school. When the short-lived marriage ended, she was left with a child. She felt lost, abandoned.

She walked the city streets, day and night, aimlessly. For a length of time she thought she was too far gone to deserve asking God's help. Most days she was drinking. She was living a life of total abandon. That went on for a few years.

One day, about two in the afternoon, already tipsy from the noontime drinking, beside the street she was wandering in, she realized there was a church. She found herself whispering to herself -- "Jesus, you're my God, help me." She did not enter the church. She kept on her way.

The following weeks and months, she started to have dreams which to this day she remembers vividly. "As though they happened last night", she says. In one dream she felt the Blessed Virgin Mary touching her forehead, telling her she was forgiven. Sometimes the dream had St. Anne, the mother of Mary, also there, doing and saying the same thing. Then there was a dream with her walking the streets aimlessly, as she did in her waking hours. But in the dream she was followed by a child, barefooted, clothed like any child playing on the sidewalks of Cebu City at that time. No matter how fast Tranquilina walked, the child kept the same distance. Finally, in the dream, she stopped, looked back and asked who he was. The child in the dream said his name was Agustin.

When she woke up from that dream, she realized that the Santo Niño is at the San Agustin Church.

She started going to church again at the San Agustin Church. One time, as the priest was raising the Host, she felt a golden light in the shape of a cross hitting her eyes for a split second. Since that time Tranquilina has straightened her life.

Tranquilina is one of those faces, the hundreds who frequently attend the First Friday prayers and all the prayers leading to the Fiestas. Since she lived in Tampa, she has never failed coming to the Fiesta celebration. Her devotion is quiet and personal. That is how she wants it.

∾

When Teresa and Mel Ebrada moved to Tampa in 1997, they immediately sought religious groups to join. Since their early years in New York and Pennsylvania, they have always found comfort in belonging to Filipino religious groups. Their inquiries from new Filipino acquaintances led them to the Santo Niño group. They have never left. Instead their involvement, like that of most members, has widened and deepened. Whenever they find time outside their professional and personal commitments, they always use it to attend the Santo Niño novena on First Fridays.

Teresa is from Maasin, Leyte, the daughter of parents who are both lawyers. She describes her mother as "very religious, goes to church daily, frequently kneeling her way from the church door to the altar." In their youth, this family of eleven siblings in the Philippines habitually prayed the rosary everyday at 6 p.m. Before every child's birthday, a Santo Niño novena would be said by the whole family. In the center of the house was a statue of Christ the King. This was the first image everyone who entered the house would see, and the last image seen as one leaves.

With this kind of religious environment, it would be inevitable that at least one or two would go to a religious community. A brother did become a priest whose extraordinary talents made him Prefect at the University of Santo Tomas Seminary in Manila. But he decided to dedicate his priestly ministry to community and social problems. He was in the United States working with fishermen on environmental issues when, in 1998, he died aboard the plane on his way to a project.

When Teresa arrived in New York to start her nursing career, she felt lonely and afraid like anyone suddenly thrown to an unfamiliar place. She remembered what her mother used to tell each one of them – "Everything is God's will. Plan everything with God." She kept praying to the Santo Niño. She also frequented the Carmelite church in Manhattan. One day, she asked one of the church workers where she could buy a scapular. Suddenly there was a woman who looked like she could be a Filipina although her name sounded Chinese. She offered Teresa lots of scapulars. The woman suggested that they be given to anyone interested, which Teresa did, even sending some to the Philippines. Teresa tried to call her to extend the gratitude from all those who received the scapular but she never got an answer. She never saw the woman again.

Teresa's husband Mel Ebrada, familiar to most Santo Niño devotees being frequently at the First Friday devotions and also one of the lead bearers of the Santo Niño caro during the Fiestas, is from Pontevedra, Negros Occidental. He says that he did not come from a religious family although he was raised a Catholic. "I was one of the Doubting Thomases", he says, "a seasonal Catholic". After they got married Teresa got him to become more devoted. In addition to their close involvement with the Santo Niño Devotion, they have been in Couples for Christ for 8 years now. In Pennsylvania they were in the Charismatic Movement.

Their love story is one for the movies too. Mel, an engineer, was working in Saudi Arabia with Teresa's brother from whom he first saw her picture. He started communicating with her. Later, he visited her in Manila. When Teresa came to the U.S. in 1983, Mel in Saudi was told by Teresa's brother – "You better join Teresa in the U.S. She might marry an American." Mel did not need to be told twice. As soon as he could, he left Saudi to join Teresa in New York. They got married and later lived in Pennsylvania.

The tales we tell, sooner or later, is about love, human and Divine. But one, inevitably, is part of the other.

◔

The story that Sylvia Gogo tells illustrates that when we are spared the loss of priced possessions that too is a blessing. Sylvia and Prospero, a retired nurse and pediatrician respectively, are recent transfers to the Tampa Bay Area from Beckley, West Virginia. Their becoming part of the Santo Niño Devotion is another illustration of how the chain reaction of friendships strengthens the Devotion. When they moved to this area, they already had a set of close friends living here who belong to the Santo Niño Devotion.

Sylvia herself was raised to be devoted to the Santo Niño since childhood. "As far as praying goes," she says now, "about the way a child prays, I remember that it was easier to talk to a Child." She meant herself as a child talking to another child, the Santo Niño, which she saw as a friend. Like most of the Devotees, Sylvia grew up in a home with a Santo Niño statue. She carries always a small Santo Niño image. In all her homes in America, the statue has a special niche.

Sometime in late 2009, when they were out of town, their home was burglarized. Many valuables were lost. But spared were precious jewelries and heirlooms. Sylvia sees this as a Santo Niño miracle. These particular valuables were on a shelf inside a walk-in closet. Right in front of this closet is their home altar with a Santo Niño statue. The thieves opened every hiding place they have except the walk-in closet. Sylvia believes that somehow the closet door was made invisible to the thieves, that it appeared to them as a plain wall. She concludes this as an intervention by the Santo Niño because His statue is right in front of the closet door.

◔

Alice Kuntz and her husband Chuck are part of the group in the mid-1990s who faithfully, patiently did their part in building the Santo Niño Devotion to its present state. They have not stop doing that.

Alice's story is that whenever she prays to the Blessed Mother, she sees different visions of her – as a shadow, a bright light, an actual outline such as seen in church images. Alice is a firm believer that in the intensity of prayers and devotion, the devotee is granted visions. She has always been a Santo Niño devotee even when she was still in the Philippines.

∾

Such are our stories. It is in our nature to humanize the Divine whose interventions we constantly seek. The wish that Whom we worship takes on a human form with our wit, wisdom and wiliness, creates the stories that turn into legends and myths.

The Santo Niño, especially in Cebu, is rich with these stories. There's the one about "a short, very dark, curly haired little boy" who stands beside the San Agustin church and gets fish from passing vendors, charging it to the church personnel. When the vendors come back to get their money, the church authorities are baffled -- no one is authorized to buy fish, much less a little boy. Later, they find well-wrapped fish beside the Santo Niño image in the altar. Another common story is that of the Santo Niño as a wanderer. Countless are the recorded claims of finding the statue of the Santo Niño on early mornings with mud on His shoes, grass stains on His cape, and His garments wet, coated with sand and smelling of the sea. There's the story of a drunken altar custodian who got tired of cleaning the Santo Niño's vestments and said "Since you love to wander at night, why don't you bring me some money?" Lo and behold, the next morning, beside the muddy shoes of the Santo Niño, was some cash. Equally innumerable are the stories of the Santo Niño saving towns all over the Philippines from war invaders, floods, typhoons, fires and other natural disasters.

Divine Interventions come unlabeled and uncategorized. It is for us to sort it out and file into our own personal earthly classification, depending on what human need we wanted the Intervention to alleviate.

What we call blessings serve us in many ways -- guiding our thoughts and decisions to take us to a better place, saving us from mortal and spiritual danger, even keeping valued material possessions from being lost. Earthly creatures that we are, we invoke Heavenly Graces to protect our animate and inanimate acquisitions.

Praying that we be spared from earthly harm is a recognition and an admission of our fears that we are always exposed to countless hurtful things. Each time we are left unharmed from all those "thousand natural shocks that flesh is heir to" we call it a blessing, an answer to some prayer. It then becomes another story to tell.

This Friendship, this Devotion, this Family, took shape because we prayed, we talked, we listened. We shared the stories of our vulnerabilities, our ideas of salvation, our narrow escapes, our noble and petty selves, our inspirations and moments of despair.

So here we are, a Family, the bearers and the unofficial missionaries of the Santo Niño Devotion. As we continue to spread the Santo Niño Story with our stories, we can only hope that we tell them with heart and Grace.

29

Seeking A Second Shore

The night deepens. The darkness outside makes the quiet feel solid as though a curtain has dropped around him. The passing cars on Dale Mabry are few and far between, muted in their passing. Even at this late hour, people are going places, leaving places. Journeys, this is what it's all about. This is what we are all about. His own journey? Who knows. He gazes intently at the brightly lighted Santo Niño statue.

Since childhood he has noticed that when he stares at a church statue long enough, it slowly looks less wooden, its contours soften. His unblinking gaze turns the saintly faces fleshly soft. He can almost see the fine pulsations of a living being aware of his presence. Many moments in his life, he has asked himself -- When we pray, do we expect to see movement in whomever we are praying to, to get a sense that there is a life listening, perceiving our presence?

The silhouette of a tree under a lighted post outside the Shrine is reflected on the glass enclosure of the Santo Niño statue. It gives a surreal effect of the Santo Niño rising above trees, above the world, a vigilant Guardian.

Then he sees a small Santo Niño statue left on one of the Shrine's granite benches. It lies on its side, a carved miniature of a child overcome with sleep. On taking a closer look, he sees that the statue has a missing left arm. Beside it is a lone flower, still with its stem, but withering, left over from some bouquet offered at the Sinulog dance hours ago. Beside the withered blossom is the severed arm of the Santo Niño statue still attached to its globe. He picks up the Santo Niño statue. He picks up the severed arm. He leaves the withered flower at the foot of the brightly lighted Shrine Santo Niño. He puts the armless Santo Niño and its severed arm in his pocket. He walks to the dark outside.

In dreams begin responsibility.

— *W. B. Yeats*